TRADE ISSUES, POLICIES AND LAWS

FREIGHT MOBILITY AND CONNECTIVITY IN CHINA AND U.S. TRADE ISSUES

TRADE ISSUES, POLICIES AND LAWS

Additional books in this series can be found on Nova's website under the Series tab.

Additional e-books in this series can be found on Nova's website under the e-book tab.

TRADE ISSUES, POLICIES AND LAWS

FREIGHT MOBILITY AND CONNECTIVITY IN CHINA AND U.S. TRADE ISSUES

LILLIAN EMMETT
EDITOR

nova publishers
New York

For permission to use material from this book please contact us:
Telephone 631-231-7269; Fax 631-231-8175
Web Site: http://www.novapublishers.com

Library of Congress Cataloging-in-Publication Data

ISBN: 978-1-63321-422-4

Published by Nova Science Publishers, Inc. † New York

CONTENTS

PREFACE

This book discusses the freight mobility and intermodal connectivity in China as well as provides an overview of U.S.-China commercial relations, including major trade disputes.

Chapter 1 – Trade growth between the United States and China has increased U.S. interest in how the Chinese transportation system handles exports. The Federal Highway Administration, American Association of State Highway and Transportation Officials, and National Cooperative Highway Research Program sponsored a scanning study to identify how China provides intermodal access to its ports and uses investment strategies to foster freight mobility and intermodal connectivity.

The scan team learned that China's national, provincial, and metropolitan transportation policy is closely coordinated with the country's economic policy and social harmony goals. The transportation system is expanding rapidly to meet global intermodal freight demands and promote expansion into underdeveloped regions of the country.

Team recommendations for U.S. implementation include reviving a national transportation infrastructure focus to maintain U.S. competitiveness in the global market, conducting a study on how China uses performance measures to manage transportation policy, and synthesizing the results of this and earlier scans on intermodal freight and connectivity around the world.

Chapter 2 – U.S.-China economic ties have expanded substantially over the past three decades. Total U.S.-China trade rose from $2 billion in 1979 to $562 billion in 2013. China is currently the United States' second-largest trading partner, its third-largest export market, and its biggest source of imports. China is estimated to be a $300 billion market for U.S. firms (based on U.S. exports to China and sales by U.S.-invested firms in China). Many

U.S. firms view participation in China's market as critical to staying globally competitive. General Motors (GM), for example, which has invested heavily in China, sold more cars in China than in the United States each year from 2010 to 2013. In addition, U.S. imports of low-cost goods from China greatly benefit U.S. consumers, and U.S. firms that use China as the final point of assembly for their products, or use Chinese-made inputs for production in the United States, are able to lower costs. China is the largest foreign holder of U.S. Treasury securities ($1.3 trillion as of November 2013). China's purchases of U.S. government debt help keep U.S. interest rates low.

Despite growing commercial ties, the bilateral economic relationship has become increasingly complex and often fraught with tension. From the U.S. perspective, many trade tensions stem from China's incomplete transition to a free market economy. While China has significantly liberalized its economic and trade regimes over the past three decades, it continues to maintain (or has recently imposed) a number of state-directed policies that appear to distort trade and investment flows. Major areas of concern expressed by U.S. policy makers and stakeholders include China's relatively poor record of intellectual property rights (IPR) enforcement and alleged widespread cyber espionage against U.S. firms by Chinese government entities; its mixed record on implementing its World Trade Organization (WTO) obligations; its extensive use of industrial policies (such as financial support of state-owned firms, trade and investment barriers, and pressure on foreign-invested firms in China to transfer technology in exchange for market access) in order to promote the development of industries favored by the government and protect them from foreign competition; and its policies to maintain an undervalued currency. Many U.S. policy makers argue that such policies harm U.S. economic interests and have contributed to U.S. job losses. For example, one study estimated that Chinese IPR infringement cost the U.S. economy up to $240 billion annually. There are a number of views in the United States over how to more effectively address commercial disputes with China:

- Take a more aggressive stand against China, such as increasing the number of dispute settlement cases brought against China in the WTO, or threatening to impose trade sanctions against China unless it addresses policies (such as IPR theft) that hurt U.S. economic interests.
- Intensify negotiations through existing high-level bilateral dialogues, such as the U.S.-China Strategic & Economic Dialogue (S&ED), which was established to discuss long-term challenges in the

relationship. In addition, seek to complete ongoing U.S. negotiations with China to reach a high-standard bilateral investment treaty (BIT), as well as to finalize negotiations in the WTO toward achieving China's accession to the Government Procurement Agreement (GPA).

- Encourage China to join the Trans-Pacific Partnership (TPP) negotiations and/or seek to negotiate a bilateral a free trade agreement (FTA) with China.
- Continue to press China to implement comprehensive economic reforms, such as diminishing the role of the state in the economy and implementing policies to boost domestic consumption.

Economic and trade reforms begun in 1979 have helped transform China into one of the world's fastest-growing economies. China's economic growth and trade liberalization, including comprehensive trade commitments made upon entering the World Trade Organization (WTO) in 2001, have led to a sharp expansion in U.S.-China commercial ties. Yet, bilateral trade relations have become increasingly strained in recent years over a number of issues, including a large and growing U.S. trade deficit with China, resistance by China to appreciate its currency to market levels, China's mixed record on implementing its WTO obligations, infringement of U.S. intellectual property (including through cyber espionage), and numerous Chinese industrial policies that appear to impose new restrictions on foreign firms or provide unfair advantages to domestic Chinese firms (such as subsidies). Several Members of Congress have called on the Obama Administration to take a tougher stance against China to induce it to eliminate trade and economic policies deemed harmful to U.S. economic interests and/or inconsistent with WTO rules. This report provides an overview of U.S.-China commercial relations, including major trade disputes.

In: Freight Mobility and Connectivity … ISBN: 978-1-63321-422-4
Editor: Lillian Emmett

Chapter 1

FREIGHT MOBILITY AND INTERMODAL CONNECTIVITY IN CHINA*

David Cole, Tony Furst, Sharon Daboin, Warren Hoemann, Michael Meyer, Richard Nordahl, Marygrace Parker, Leo Penne, Norman Stoner and Tianjia Tang

ABSTRACT

Trade growth between the United States and China has increased U.S. interest in how the Chinese transportation system handles exports. The Federal Highway Administration, American Association of State Highway and Transportation Officials, and National Cooperative Highway Research Program sponsored a scanning study to identify how China provides intermodal access to its ports and uses investment strategies to foster freight mobility and intermodal connectivity.

The scan team learned that China's national, provincial, and metropolitan transportation policy is closely coordinated with the country's economic policy and social harmony goals. The transportation system is expanding rapidly to meet global intermodal freight demands and promote expansion into underdeveloped regions of the country.

---

* This is an edited, reformatted and augmented version of report number, FHWA-PL-08-020, issued by the Office of International Programs, Federal Highway Administration, U.S. Department of Transportation, May 2008.

Team recommendations for U.S. implementation include reviving a national transportation infrastructure focus to maintain U.S. competitiveness in the global market, conducting a study on how China uses performance measures to manage transportation policy, and synthesizing the results of this and earlier scans on intermodal freight and connectivity around the world.

EXECUTIVE SUMMARY

China's transportation system is rapidly expanding to support economic growth, meet projected global intermodal freight demands, and promote expansion into underdeveloped regions of the country. Given the current understanding of intermodal freight movement that was not available when the United States developed its port capacity, the purpose of this scan was to identify how China provides intermodal access to its new, greenfield maritime ports and the possible application of those methods in the United States. The scan also looked at the investment strategies adopted by Chinese officials to foster freight mobility and intermodal connectivity in support of their global competitiveness.

The scan team represented a diverse set of interests and concerns for national and State decisionmaking. In addition to Federal Highway Administration (FHWA) officials at the national and division levels, the team included representatives from the departments of transportation for California, Maine, and Pennsylvania; a representative of the I-95 Corridor Coalition; a representative of the American Association of State Highway and Transportation Officials (AASHTO); a representative of the American Trucking Associations; and a university professor who also acted as the report writer. These scan members reflected different modal interests and expertise in intermodal freight transportation, trucking, transportation policy and planning, and transportation system operations.

The scan team met with government officials at the national, provincial, and metropolitan levels; port authorities and terminal operators; U.S. shippers and retailers; logistics and warehousing companies; and research organizations. Although most of the team's visits were to specific organizations, meetings were also held under the auspices of the local American Chambers of Commerce in Shanghai and Hong Kong that provided an opportunity to meet with representatives of many shipper, carrier, and trade organizations.

General Observations

The scan team made numerous observations about the way China has provided transportation infrastructure in support of its impressive economic growth. These observations are presented below. However, several major takeaways from this scan provide important lessons to the United States:

- Given the global market and supply chain, what happens in China does affect the U.S., State, and local economies. Everyone is part of a global economy; flows of people and goods do not stop at jurisdictional boundaries. Although this scan focused on China, in reality the transportation system of each country is part of a global transportation network and should be viewed that way. It is surely the way the companies that move freight view it.
- Although the Chinese system of governance is very different from the United States, several characteristics of the system are noteworthy:
    - National, provincial, and metropolitan transportation policy is closely coordinated among the three levels and is linked to other policy goals, the most prominent ones being economic development and what the Chinese call "social harmony."
    - This strong linkage often results in a unified vision of what is necessary in the transport sector to achieve policy goals.
    - The Chinese government at all levels targets investment on those components of the transportation system that best advance national goals. As a result, the evolving Chinese transportation system is focused on excelling in markets dominated by international trade.
    - The expanding opportunities for investment in China have resulted in many public-private joint ventures for transportation projects. However, in most cases, the government retains majority control in the joint venture. It always has the majority say.
- On intermodal access to the maritime ports, the scan team did not find new or different operational technology than is used in the United States or European Union. There were, however, significant differences in port operating rules because of different labor conditions and the focus on competing in a global market.

The following observations from the scan are organized in four categories: China's economic growth and driving forces; transportation infrastructure development; governmental structure, decisionmaking, and analysis; and global shipper and carrier perceptions.

China's Economic Growth and Driving Forces

1. China's economic growth over the past 10 years has been dramatic. Both government officials and private sector representatives expect this growth to continue in the foreseeable future at or near its current rate of about 10 percent per annum.
2. Although the national and local governments have invested heavily in infrastructure, much of the recent economic growth has been fueled by private investment. As different sectors of the economy have been opened to foreign investment, joint ventures and other financial partnerships have provided an institutional framework for expansion of the transportation infrastructure and the economy. Even with this foreign investment, the government is still in a dominant position on investing in the transport sector, especially in such areas as the national rail system.
3. The economic expansion of China started in the south (Pearl River Delta), moved north along the coastal area based on national economic policy, and is now pushing west in accordance with the "Go West" national government campaign. This campaign has significant implications to supply chain logistics costs and to the efficiency of the Chinese transportation system in moving exports to the coastal ports.
4. Much of China's economic expansion has occurred in urban areas where the population provides the labor force. The consequence of such large urban concentrations is that the central government pays particular attention to and provides the resources to make sure that the basic needs of these populations are met (social harmony). From a transportation perspective, the consequence of this policy focus is that passenger transportation often receives priority over freight movement (although in port cities freight movement often receives close attention from transportation officials), especially in peak holiday seasons.
5. Although it appears that economic development is still the primary goal of governmental policy, additional goals and performance measures relating to environmental quality and energy consumption have been added to the national agenda.

Transportation Infrastructure Development and Operations

1. Recognizing the vital role that transportation plays in meeting its goal of continued economic growth, China is investing heavily in transport infrastructure, an investment estimated at more than 9 percent of the country's gross domestic product (GDP). This investment comes from both public and private (joint venture) funds.
2. Substantial levels of private capital are being invested, in some cases with low expectations of rapid return on investment. In other words, investors are willing to accept lower immediate returns in exchange for longer term benefits. Over the past several years, this investment has occurred primarily in seaports, highways, airports, and logistics parks. Private investment in rail infrastructure and intermodal terminals has had limited success, although some recent agreements suggest that the rail sector will also see private investment.
3. Coastal and river shipping is a significant component of China's intermodal transportation system. In some port markets, as much as 35 percent of the containers arriving for export do so by barge.
4. The central government's "Go West" policy has shifted investment attention to inland transportation and the challenges facing such transportation, especially the connections to the major international ports.
5. China's intermodal rail service faces significant challenges. The movement of containers receives low in priority on China's rail network, following military, passenger, energy (coal), and food movements. About 12,000 kilometers (7,456 miles) of passenger-only track are being built to separate passenger and freight movements. This will free up the existing combined-use track for freight movements. A goal of 10 million 20-foot equivalent units (TEUs) carried by rail (now less than 3 million) has been established for China's current 5-year planning period.
6. The Chinese central government has encouraged joint ventures to finance the national expressway system, the intent of which is to stretch government funds to support a variety of new modal investments. Consideration is also being given in some locales to how tolls can be used to influence truck routing.
7. Toll rates are comparable to those found in the United States and Europe, but the Chinese believe this does not reflect the economic reality of travelers in China, where per capita GDP is much lower. In some cases, the Chinese are trying to renegotiate concession

agreements to allow lower toll rates, offsetting lower toll revenues with longer concession time periods (from 30 to 50 years).

8. The national expressway plan is centered primarily on three major economic and political centers: Beijing, Shanghai, and the Pearl River Delta. In essence, the national expressway system and the national rail network will be the major means of connection between the political and economic centers of the country, reinforcing their importance in the economic future of China. Intermodal connection has been an important consideration in network design.
9. Trucking is the predominant means of moving containers to and from the ports, especially in the river delta manufacturing regions. The trucking industry consists mainly of small businesses (one to three trucks), which makes its contribution to China's economic growth even more impressive. Enforcement of the standard vehicle configuration regulation is weak, and integration of technology into trucking operations appears to be limited.
10. Given the relatively large number of trucking businesses found in China and the intense competition for freight movements, it was not surprising to find that oversized and overweight trucks have become an emerging and important concern for transportation officials. It appears that Chinese transportation and enforcement organizations have just recently begun to implement national and provincial weight enforcement programs.
11. Chinese port productivity is the best in the world. Chinese ports operate 24 hours a day, 7 days a week, 365 days a year. Operational strategies are impressive—cranes that lift four TEUs, 20- to 30-minute truck turns, nine cranes working one ship, etc. New ports are being developed and the capacity of existing ports is being expanded rapidly.
12. Given the significant level of trade to the United States and current U.S. legislation, security was a growing concern to port terminal operators. The relatively new infrastructure at China's ports allows terminal operators to build security measures into terminal operations, especially using technologies to screen outbound containers.
13. China has not progressed to the point of systematically managing its transportation infrastructure; it is still in the "build" mode. The scan team saw little evidence that this infrastructure was being designed with system management challenges in mind, such as truck weight and size enforcement. Nevertheless, in a few of the more mature areas

experiencing significant congestion, transportation officials indicated a need to begin paying serious attention to system management.

14. Intermodal connectivity and landside access to Chinese ports are not approached differently or in a more sophisticated way than in the United States or European Union. Many new port facilities are located in large urban areas, yet the access to and from these ports involves traversing mixed-use roadways that will, in the future, present the same challenges now faced in the United States and European Union.
15. Rail access to maritime port facilities is not being built consistently into new port design. With the exception of the Port of Qingdao, which has no river access and is being looked at as one terminus of a rail-land bridge from Asia to the European Union and Russia, no other port facility was being built with on-dock rail. This is partly due to a perception by shippers and ocean carriers that container movement receives low priority on the Chinese freight rail network, which results in little pressure to improve or provide rail access to the ports.

Governmental Structure, Decisionmaking, and Analysis

1. China's policymaking and implementation process identifies clearly specified national goals with corresponding performance metrics. However, local officials have leeway under this national policy to implement projects that also meet their local objectives. A national 5-year plan provides policy direction on what will be emphasized during the plan's timeframe (China is in its 11th 5-year plan).
2. National transportation agencies have different modal responsibilities (e.g., Ministry of Communications,[*] Ministry of Railways, Ministry of Construction, Central Administration of Civil Aviation). Because the performance of government officials is measured by results, attention is paid to measures of progress. National data on overall modal performance and the state of the economy are collected and analyzed. Data analysis is used to determine the extent to which goals are being met at different levels of government. Some officials referred to this as "results-oriented planning."

[*] In April 2008, the Chinese government created a Ministry of Transportation that incorporates the former Ministry of Communications. Aviation, maritime, and highways are among the functions in the Ministry of Transportation. The Ministry of Railways remains separate. The result is a transportation policy and development entity similar in structure to the U.S. Department of Transportation.

3. The performance of local officials and governments is measured against national goals. For example, many noted that the most important metric for local officials is the degree to which economic growth occurs during their tenure, defined primarily as job growth. China's tax policy also supports this goal because the tax revenue from the economic activity in a province stays, for the most part, in the province.
4. Although this scan did not conduct a systematic assessment of the capability of municipal government agencies to plan and provide for transportation infrastructure and services, every meeting with local officials included the staff members responsible for each mode. In other words, all of the modes were located in one agency, which encouraged the adoption of a multimodal systems perspective when looking at regional transportation investment.
5. In most cases, there was little evidence that carriers or shippers were asked for advice on national strategic transportation plans or investments. However, at the provincial or regional level, the inclusion of the private sector in tactical investment decisions was evident in the number of public-private partnerships.
6. Port development plans considered modal access strategies as part of the planning process, but multimodal port access did not always result (note comment 15 in the previous section about rail access to ports). The interesting aspect of this port planning was that the boundary of such studies encompassed a much larger area than that adjacent to the port itself. Access was a key concern.
7. Project development occurs much faster in China than in the United States. Transportation projects are viewed as a priority for economic development, so they move forward rapidly.
8. In keeping with the national policy of social harmony, government officials are concerned about the negative impacts of transportation facility operations and expansion on local communities. They provided examples of efforts to mitigate the impact when community displacement does occur.
9. Hong Kong's role in the competitive market of the Pearl River Delta is evolving. New ports nearby (along with dredging in the river to allow access to these ports for bigger ships), as well as new manufacturing development on the west bank of the Pearl River, will likely cause a shift in container exports to other ports. It remains to be seen how the market will adjust to these changing conditions, but it

appears that Hong Kong's relative position in global container flows could evolve in a different direction in the future.

Shipper and Carrier Perceptions

1. Many of the international ocean carriers and shippers the team met during this scan view the serious constraint in international trade and supply chain efficiency as being on the receiving end, in Europe and the United States. The prevalent perception is that terminal throughput in the United States and European Union is limited by terminal operational limitations, landside access capacity, growing road congestion, and protracted decisionmaking processes.
2. Shippers and carriers believe that the effect of a widened Panama Canal and increased transits through the Suez Canal will likely be more shipments heading to east coast U.S. ports, but that the west coast U.S. ports will still be the major destination for most transpacific containers.
3. Several shippers and carriers identified the "bunching" of vessel departures from Chinese ports (because of when merchandise arrives at the ports and when it is needed in the U.S. market) as the cause of a significant peaking problem. It was observed that a peaking in departures from China usually results in a peaking in arrivals at U.S. ports, especially Los Angeles-Long Beach in California. Several shippers and carriers believe that this peaking phenomenon could be remedied by working with retailers, shippers, and manufacturers.

Lessons for the United States

The lessons learned from this scan are organized in two major categories: consequences to the United States and its transportation system, and different approaches to planning and project development in support of a growing economy.

> "Whereas the United States focuses on China...China focuses on the world."
>
> – Scan Team Member

Consequences to the United States and the U.S. Transportation System

1. China competes as a nation. For the United States to remain competitive globally, it needs to invest in transportation infrastructure, apply new system management technologies, and consider institutional change in how it identifies, funds, operates, and makes key infrastructure improvements to key elements of the national transportation system.
2. Trade from China will put increasing pressure on east coast ports. With new service routes through the Suez and Panama Canals, States on the east coast will experience increasing demands on their transportation systems.
3. Given the navigable draft and terminal capacity of most U.S. ports, the largest container ships might not be providing service to the United States. This means most U.S. ports will be served by vessels carrying less than or equal to 10,000 TEUs.
4. Similar to what teams observed during intermodal freight scans in Europe and Latin America, the difference in port efficiency between China and the United States is dramatic. If U.S. ports are unable to expand because of community concerns or geographic limitations, maximizing the use of existing capacity and improving port throughput are imperative to handle increasing container flows.
5. The United States can learn a lot from China on using natural geography to the maximum extent, particularly in the use of barge and coastal shipping as access modes to major ports. In China, the Pearl and Yangtze River ports are being developed to act as transshipment ports, and new manufacturing capacity is being developed and located to take advantage of river transport.
6. Freight bottlenecks are viewed as a drain on transportation system and economic productivity. This is a perspective the United States should adopt as well. Solving these bottlenecks involves more than just expanding physical capacity. It also requires using technology and operational strategies.
7. Chinese officials have recognized that freight-oriented transportation investments, especially ports, are an important part of the nation's economic development. Accordingly, Chinese transportation agencies have invested heavily in improving port capacity.
8. The United States is fortunate to have a much more developed rail network, which in many cases provides on-dock service to port

terminals. This is a significant advantage to U.S. trade flows, and one that needs to be nurtured.

9. Given China's experience with oversize and overweight vehicles and the corresponding infrastructure damage, it becomes even more apparent that the United States should ensure that its commercial motor vehicle size and weight program continues to advance and is provided adequate resources.
10. One challenge facing west coast ports is the bunching of vessel departures from China that results in vessels arriving at about the same time in the United States. If vessel bunching could be reduced, this could significantly benefit both U.S. and Chinese ports. In discussions with shippers and carriers in China, the scan team heard optimism that this could in fact occur.

How the Chinese Invest in and Operate Their Transportation System to Support a Growing Economy

1. China has a national transportation investment policy that is closely linked to its trade and economic policy. National transportation investment appears to focus on two major goals (besides military defense): strategies to foster social harmony among Chinese citizens and strategies to support economic growth, with the second goal supporting the first. The United States would benefit from adopting a national transportation investment policy that supports the nation's economic health.
2. The Chinese central planning function is not a model that would work in the United States. However, the concept of locally executing a strategic network focused on national interests with national financing support (along the lines of the initial effort to build the U.S. Interstate Highway System) is worth considering. Such a system should use performance measures to monitor progress in developing and operating key elements of the national transportation system.
3. Many of the assets that work in tandem with the Chinese transportation system (port terminal development, logistics parks, etc.) are partially funded through private investment. In some cases, the return on this investment is not likely to be realized in the short term. Instead, it will take years for the investment to start producing net gains. However, companies made it clear that because the Chinese can make infrastructure investment decisions quickly and show progress toward improvement, they are willing to invest. This

suggests that if transportation agencies in the United States are interested in encouraging more private investment in transportation facilities, they need to give greater attention to timely public sector decisionmaking. Agencies simply need to get to the decision point earlier.
4. The primary instrument of privatization in China is the joint venture. In almost all cases, private investors do not get a majority share of the investment (the exception being port terminals). Government agencies or state-owned enterprises retain at least 51 percent control.
5. Chinese planning for intermodal centers, and indeed for regional transportation networks, adopts a systems perspective on performance and investment. In the United States, several multistate coalitions seek to coordinate multi-jurisdictional activity. To achieve systems-level coordination, more efforts along these lines will be necessary.
6. Air cargo is the fastest growing segment of freight movement in China. While it is still only a small percentage of total tonnage, the implication to the U.S. transportation system of this growth in both air cargo hubs and belly freight is new stress on the transportation network at already-overcrowded U.S. airports.
7. National data collection in China provides a springboard for national transportation planning, investment, and performance evaluation. U.S. freight data systems should not only be continued, but expanded to provide the information needed for optimal transportation investment decisionmaking, especially given the important role that freight plays in the economic health of the Nation.
8. Finally, it was noteworthy that the Chinese transportation officials who met with the scan team were very high quality professionals and most often quite young. They were expert in the use of data and data analysis and knowledgeable about how their respective transportation systems fit into a much larger transportation systems perspective.

Implementation Strategies, Dissemination, and Recommendations

The scan team developed recommendations for implementing the results of this scan. These related to dissemination, policy development, outreach, and research and data analysis activities. For example, the scan team recommends a wakeup call on the need for the United States to invest in transportation infrastructure with a more national perspective if it is to stay competitive in a global market. This first, and perhaps most important, recommendation is to develop a "Reveille for Refocus" on a fresh, strategic, national perspective for U.S. transportation and elected officials. This document would draw a sharp focus on the importance of the transportation-economic integration so evident in China. More discussion of the implementation plan is in the report.

SECTION 1: INTRODUCTION

China has been a major trading partner with the United States for many years. This relationship is likely to become even stronger in the future. The success of this trading relationship very much depends on the efficiency and productivity of freight movements between the two countries and the logistics system that supports such movements. With an increasing volume of imports coming into the United States from China, the ability of the Chinese transportation system to handle its exports is of great interest to U.S. transportation officials. The ability of the U.S. transportation system to handle these volumes on the receiving end is also important—and cause for concern. The Chinese government has invested heavily in transportation, with much of this investment coming from private investors. The United States can learn from this experience.

China's transportation system is rapidly expanding to support economic growth, meet projected global intermodal freight demands, and promote expansion into underdeveloped regions of the country. Given the current understanding of intermodal freight movement that was not available when the United States developed its port capacity, the purpose of this scan was to identify how China provides intermodal access to its new, greenfield maritime ports and the possible application of those methods in the United States. The scan also looked at the investment strategies adopted by Chinese officials to foster freight mobility and intermodal connectivity in support of their global competitiveness.

Scan Composition

The scan team represented a diverse set of interests and concerns for national and State decisionmaking (see appendix A for scan team member biographies). In addition to Federal Highway Administration (FHWA) officials at the national and division levels, the team included representatives from the departments of transportation for California, Maine, and Pennsylvania; a representative of the I-95 Corridor Coalition; a representative of the American Association of State Highway and Transportation Officials (AASHTO); a representative of the American Trucking Associations; and a university professor who also acted as the report writer. These scan members represented different modal interests and expertise in intermodal freight transportation, trucking, transportation policy and planning, and transportation system operations.

The scan team met with the following groups during its 15-day trip:

- Ministry of Communications (intercity highways, airports, and ports)*
- China Railway Container Corp. (organization under the Ministry of Railways)
- Provincial officials and representatives of the Hong Kong Special Administrative Region
- Port authorities
- Port terminal operators
- Ocean carriers
- Municipalities (Shanghai, Shenzhen, and Qingdao)
- U.S. shippers and retailers
- Logistics and warehousing firms
- China Development Institute

Although most of the team's visits were to specific organizations, meetings were also held under the auspices of the local American Chambers of Commerce in Shanghai and Hong Kong. The meetings provided an opportunity to meet with individuals representing many different shipper, carrier, and trade organizations.

In preparation for the scan, the team sent a set of amplifying questions (see Appendix B) to the organizations it planned to visit to outline the type of information desired.

* In April 2008, the Chinese government created a Ministry of Transportation that incorporates the former Ministry of Communications. Aviation, maritime, and highways are among the functions in the Ministry of Transportation. The Ministry of Railways remains separate. The result is a transportation policy and development entity similar in structure to the U.S. Department of Transportation.

Report Organization

This report is organized in five sections. Section 2 discusses the special circumstances that reflect the Chinese experience with infrastructure provision, the expansion of the Chinese economy over the past decades, and the implications to the transportation system. Section 3 describes China's investments in transportation and plans for the future, and presents observations from private company representatives who met with the scan team. Sections 4 and 5 present general observations, lessons for the United States, and recommendations for implementing the scan results.

SECTION 2: CHINESE CONTEXT

It is often difficult to compare the United States to other countries because of differing governmental structures, patterns of economic development, and positions in the global marketplace. This is especially true in any comparison between China and the United States. This section describes the key contextual differences between the two countries that should be considered when drawing conclusions or making observations on the characteristics of respective transportation system investment or productivity.

Stage of Development

China is in a very different stage of development than the United States. In essence, China is building a transportation network in 10 years comparable to what the United States did in 50 years, and it is doing so by learning lessons from more developed countries. Opening the Chinese market to foreign investment in the late 1980s and 1990s was a calculated step by the central Chinese government to speed up the process of modernizing and developing economic linkages to the rest of the world. Thus, the fact that China is investing almost 10 percent of its gross domestic product (GDP) in all of its infrastructure (compared to just under 4 percent in the United States) and that the Chinese economy is expanding at more than 10 percent a year (compared to 2 to 3 percent in the United States) should not be surprising.

China's rapid economic development has been reflected in the significant investment in the nation's transportation system. As this report shows, China has devoted considerable resources and has attracted much more private investment to its transportation system. China is directing almost all of the funding to new construction, while paying little apparent attention to incorporating aspects of systems management into facility design (such as weigh-in-motion technologies). In the United States and Europe, transportation agencies are now learning that thinking about systems operations and management in the early stages of network development saves time and resources later when such technologies must be retrofitted onto the network.

Governmental Structure for Decisionmaking

China has a very different form of government and decisionmaking process than the United States. With a strong centralized government and central planning authority, much of what happens in China is strongly influenced by central government policy. There are also significant differences in landownership and how land is transferred to private developers by lease instead of purchase.

Figure 1 shows the organizational structure of different levels of government in China. The Central Party Committee (CPC) is the most important participant in the broad policymaking process in China, providing leadership to the National People's Congress, State Council, and Chinese People's Political Consultative Conference. The CPC establishes national policy and often plays a critical role in making sure adopted policies are carried out. This is done primarily by having party members serve as heads of agencies (at the national level) or by having at least a party member and an administrator serve jointly as agency head (at the local level). Ministries and commissions report to the State Council. All ministries must submit an infrastructure development plan to the National Development and Reform Commission (NDRC) for approval. Table 1 shows the roles of the different groups involved in Chinese infrastructure policy, planning, and implementation.

The following are the most important transportation-related ministries:

- **Ministry of Communications**—Responsible for national roads and highways, inland waterways, ports, and ocean shipping
- **Ministry of Railways**—Responsible for the national railway system
- **Ministry of Construction**—Responsible for urban planning and urban transport

- **Central Administration of Central Aviation**—Responsible for planning and developing airports

At the provincial and municipal levels, each government has its own transportation agency, often with responsibility for all modes of transportation.

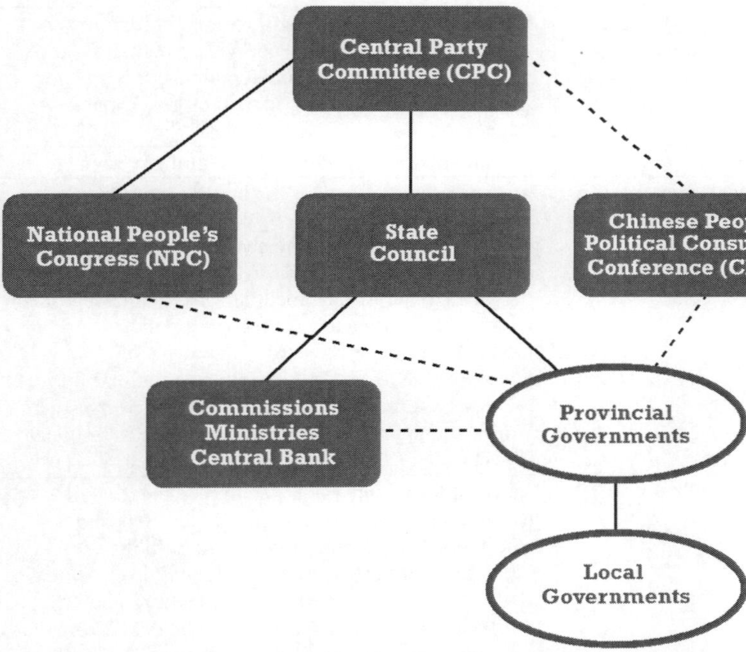

Source: Liu, Z., "Planning and Policy Coordination in China's Infrastructure Development," Paper prepared for the ADB-JBIC-World Bank East Asia Pacific Infrastructure Flagship Study, undated.

Figure 1. Chinese governmental structure.

Table 1. Role and responsibilities of relevant national Chinese organizations in infrastructure provision

Organization	Role and Responsibilities Relevant to Infrastructure
Central Party Committee	Sets national development policy direction and general guidance on long-term and medium-term national socioeconomic development plans.
National People's Congress	The national legislative body. Three of its committees are relevant to infrastructure policies and laws: Legislative Affairs, Finance and Economy, and

Table 1. (Continued)

Organization	Role and Responsibilities Relevant to Infrastructure
	Environment and Resources. It reviews and approves national economic and social development plans, the national budget, and investment megaprojects such as the Three Gorges Dam.
Chinese People's Political Consultative Conference	A multiparty advisory board, with main functions in political consultation and supervision on major political, economic, and social policies. It is a major channel for constructive criticism of government policies.
State Council	The administrative body of the central government.
National Development and Reform Commission	Formulates and organizes the implementation of national socioeconomic development strategy, long-term plan, medium-term plan (i.e., 5-year plan), and annual plan. Provides policy recommendations for macroeconomic management and sectoral development of national significance. Coordinates policy implementation across sectors and levels of government. Sets and guides implementation of price policies. Determines the size of fixed-asset investment. Guides and approves major infrastructure investment projects.
Ministry of Finance	Formulates and supervises the implementation of medium-term and annual budget plans. Sets and supervises the implementation of fiscal policies. Supervises central government expenditures. Allocates funds to central government investment projects. Sets public debt policy and manages public debt. Formulates state debt issuance plans.
People's Bank of China (Central Bank)	Analyzes, formulates, and implements macro financial credit policy based on national socio-economic development policy and sectoral policy.
Ministry of Communi-cations (now Ministry of Transportation)	Ministry responsible for roads and highways, inland waterway, ports, and ocean shipping.
Ministry of Railways	Ministry responsible for railways.
Ministry of Construction	Ministry responsible for urban planning, urban development and construction, urban utilities, and urban transport.
Ministry of Information Industry	Ministry responsible for information and telecommunications industry.
Ministry of Land and Resources	Ministry for planning, protecting, and managing the use of, land, mineral, and maritime resources.
Civil Aviation Administration of China	Central level bureau for civil aviation.

Organization	Role and Responsibilities Relevant to Infrastructure
State Environmental Protection Administration	Sets guidelines for project environmental impact assessment.
State-Owned Asset Supervision and Administration Commission of the State Council	A special agency established in 2003 under the State Council to supervise and manage the state- owned enterprises (SOEs) (including the infrastructure sector SOEs such as China Power Grid Co.) and SOE reform and restructuring.
China Development Bank	A policy bank reporting to the State Council that is heavily involved in infrastructure financing.
State Commercial Banks	Responsible for infrastructure financing and SOE financing.
Development Research Center of the State Council	An in-house think tank for the Sate Council, focusing on the overall, comprehensive, strategic, and long-term issues in the national economic and social development, and providing policy recommendations and consulting advice. Among its research departments are three highly relevant to infrastructure: Development Strategy and Regional Economy, Sectoral Economy, and Technology Economy (survey and study on major construction projects and regional development projects).
China International Engineering Consulting Corporation	The primary agency designated for the due diligence of the feasibility studies of key investment projects that require NDRC approval. It provides its services mainly on commission from project sponsors, including governments at all levels and enterprises.
Institute of Geography, China Academy of Sciences	Heavily involved in regional planning, regional urban system planning, and detailed surveys of natural resources across the country and assessment of their economic potential.

Source: Liu, Z., "Planning and Policy coordination in china's Infrastructure Development," Paper prepared for the ADB-JBIc-World Bank east Asia Pacific Infrastructure Flagship Study, undated.

Transportation Planning

Infrastructure planning in China is really a combination of top-down and bottom-up processes. The national government provides its vision for national infrastructure through the development of 5-year plans. The current 5-year plan, the 11th in the series, covers 2006–2010. Policies and targets in the plan relating to transportation include the following:

- The target for economic growth was to be 7.5 percent a year.
- National policy was aimed at supporting an economic expansion in the western provinces of China.
- Logistics was for the first time identified as a national issue, with reducing logistics cost defined as a governmental objective.
- Six new rail lines totaling 17,000 kilometers (km) (10,563 miles (mi)), six railway transportation hubs, 18 intermodal yards, 40 container handling stations, 150 intermodal substations, and 1 million km (621,371 mi) of rural roads were to be built.
- A 10 percent market share for rail intermodal traffic was established.
- All cities with more than 1 million people and 90 percent of cities with 200,000 to 1 million people were to be connected to the national road network.

The following ports were identified as being of national significance and thus needing improvements in port access and port infrastructure (see figure 7 for the locations of these port areas):

- **Yangtze River Delta**—Shanghai and Ningbo
- **Pearl River Delta**—Shenzhen and Guangzhou
- **Bohai Region**—Dalian, Tianjin, and Qingdao

Within the construct of the 5-year plan, local officials appeared to have some flexibility in investing in transportation infrastructure that meets national goals while satisfying their jurisdictional needs.

Scan team discussions with national transportation officials emphasized the cooperative nature of transportation investment, whereas local decisions were described as being much more targeted at increasing the jurisdiction's competitive advantage. Thus, local officials appeared to have a great deal of flexibility in targeting transportation investment in ways that best meet their needs.

The scan team met with representatives from several provincial and metropolitan transportation organizations. It was difficult to determine exactly how these organizations were structured, but it was notable that almost all modal planning functions were found within the government agency. This appeared to foster a multimodal perspective on transportation planning. Figure 2 for example, was presented as an illustration of how the Pearl River Delta economic and transportation system worked.

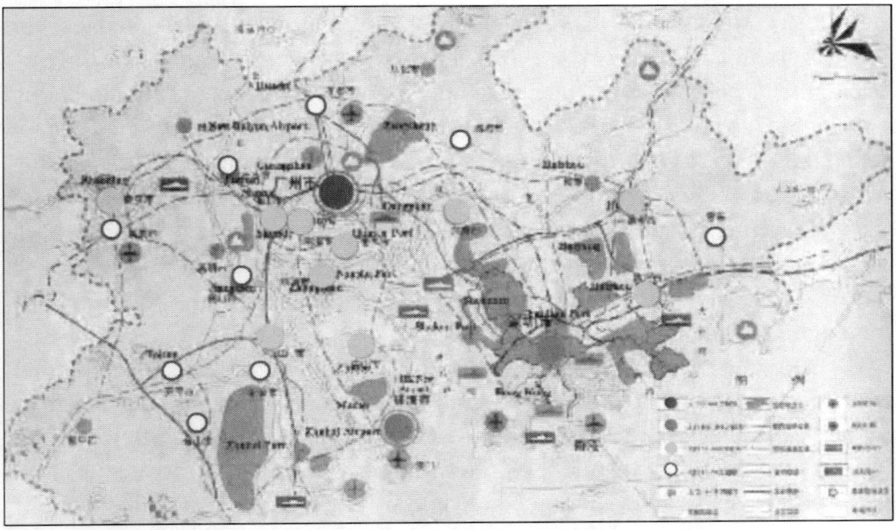

Source: Charles Guowen Wang, China Development Institute.

Figure 2. Multimodal transportation system in the Pearl River Delta.

The different symbols represent economic activities and transportation facilities. The map shows logistics corridors through which large freight volumes flow, connecting to the ports, airports, and river and barge terminals.

Transportation Investment and Finance

China has seen a profound change in its infrastructure financing strategy over the past 20 years, and not just in transportation. In 1981, for example, 57 percent of all infrastructure finance in China was funded directly by the national government through its general budget. By 1997, this had declined to 6 percent. By this date, most infrastructure was financed either through foreign direct investment, user fees, state debt, or loans from the China Development Bank.

China joined the World Trade Organization in 2001, with commitments to liberalize certain sectors of its market by set deadlines. In transportation, the government established a timetable for allowing foreign investment in different sectors. For example, in December 2002, the Ministry of Communications established a policy that foreign investment can reach 75 percent in road transport enterprise joint ventures (that is, joint ventures relating to trucking firms, warehousing, and trucking terminals). For investments that relate to roads, bridges, and other large-scale infrastructure development, foreign investment is limited to 49 percent, thus maintaining government control. This is referred to as asset equitization versus asset monetization (in which the public sector gets money from selling or leasing infrastructure). Some flexibility is allowed in increasing the private share of a joint venture under special circumstances. For example, private investment in facilities or services that serve the targeted western provinces of China can exceed the 75 percent maximum with permission of the Ministry of Communications.

Because of the many different means of investing in transportation infrastructure in China, the transportation financing picture in China can be confusing to the outsider. Data from the national ministries often do not represent the overall investment picture in logistics-related infrastructure. Rail and airport investment is mainly conducted by the national government; most seaports are invested in and owned by local government agencies or state-owned enterprises on behalf of government agencies. According to some local officials, investment incentives by local governments sometimes cause repetitive investment and overinvestment in logistics infrastructure (seaports, logistics parks).

In some cases, the Chinese government invests in infrastructure largely by itself (such as 18 freight intermodal yards) because it cannot interest private investors in the opportunity. In other cases, provincial or municipal governments invest in facilities in combination with private investors. In still others, joint ventures have been formed with several partners to develop and operate a facility. In many of these investment cases, the return on investment is small, but the expectation is that future demand (for example, volumes for toll roads) will provide bigger returns later on. Thus, it becomes impossible to generalize about transportation finance in China, except to say that the Chinese take advantage of any private investment dollars they are able to secure.

In summary, given the economic growth in China, the resources this places in the hands of the government, the governmental structure, the government's willingness to partner with private capital, private capital's interest in development opportunities, and the ability to use technological standards for roadway design and construction developed by the United States and European Union, it is not surprising to find that China has been able to expand its transportation infrastructure at such a rapid pace.

> "Chinese transportation officials are much more aware of the importance of logistics to their economy than American officials."
> – American Presidents Line Representative

Chinese Economic Growth

During the 30 years after the founding of the People's Republic of China in 1949, the national economy was centrally planned and largely controlled on the basis of traditional socialist principles. Beginning in 1978, and starting in rural areas, the central government began to relax some of the stringent constraints on economic growth. The results have been dramatic. Over the past 25 years, China's GDP has grown an average of more than 8 percent per year, with a 10.4 percent annual growth rate from 2002 to 2006. As table 2 shows, this growth is expected to continue at very high rates into the near future.

Growth in foreign trade has been the major factor spurring this economic growth. From 2002 to 2006, for example, the value of exports grew by 31.4 percent a year and the value of imports grew 29.5 percent annually. Much of this trade has been with the United States. Figure 3 shows the Chinese export destinations and the U.S. import origins for sea-based trade in 2006 (U.S. imports from Canada and Mexico are excluded). Although China is a dominant source of sea-based trade with the United States, the country has a much more diverse set of export destinations. Many in China expected this to continue in the future, with intra-Asian trade becoming more prominent for China than it is today.

According to officials at A.P. Moller– Maersk, a major shipping line serving the Chinese market, the major factors that have contributed to this growth include the following:

- **Privatization**—Most small and medium state-owned enterprises (SOEs) have become privatized.
- **SOE reform**—Larger SOEs have become more efficient and profit oriented because of governmental reforms.
- **Banking system and capital market reform**—China's financial system has been overhauled with the public listing of the major banks and reform of nontradable shares.
- **Urbanization**—Rapid urbanization across the country has created both an accessible labor pool and a rapidly growing consumer market.

- **Industry upgrade**—Chinese enterprises have been improving the quantity and quality of their manufacturing in an attempt to move up the value chain and produce more valuable goods.

All of the analysts who participated in the scan meetings expected China's historical economic growth to continue in the foreseeable future. One assessment concluded that GDP growth would occur at a 17.1 percent annual rate (at market exchange rates), the value of exports would grow by 19.2 percent a year and imports by 23 percent a year, China's share of the world's GDP at market exchange rates would increase from 6.32 percent in 2007 to 9.36 percent in 2011, and China's share of world exports would increase from 8.73 percent in 2007 to 13.56 percent in 2011. With China's government focusing on economic growth and targeting its policies on investments to foster growth, it appears likely that these predictions will come true.

An example of the linkage between central planning and economic development that has important implications for the Chinese transportation system is the plan the State Council's Research and Development Center developed in early 2005 that divided China into four regions (see figure 4). These regions were divided into eight economic zones:

Table 2. Forecasted economic factors for China, 2007 and 2011

	2007	2011	CAGR
GDP (US$ bn at market exchange rates)	3,320.3	6,236.5	17.1%
GDP (RMB bn at 1995 price)	18,698.0	25,817.0	8.4%
GDP per head (US$)	2,510.0	4,620.0	16.5%
Goods: export fob (US$ bn)	1,200.4	2,422.0	19.2%
Goods: import fob (US$ bn)	(891.5)	(2,059.0)	23.3%
Foreign direct investment (pledged US$ bn)	83.4	92.9	2.7%
Exchange rate (RMB/US$) average	7.62	6.45	-4.1%
Greater China Area export volume (million 40-ft equiv)	19.62	32.68	13.6%
Greater China Area import (million 40-ft equiv)	7.96	13.43	14.0%
China's Share of the World in 2011			

	2007	2011	CAGR
Share of world GDP (% at market exchange rate)	6.32	9.36	
Share of world GDP (% at PPP)	16.05	18.82	
Share of world exports (%)	8.73	13.56	

Note: Export and import volume data is from GCAMKT.
Source: EIU country forecast report, August 2007.

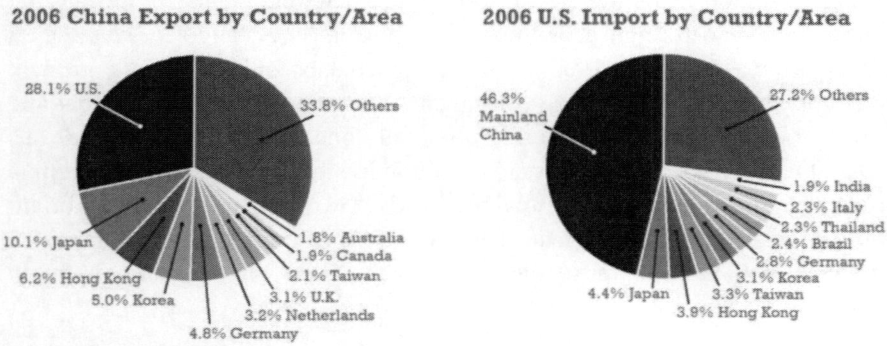

Source: A.P. Moller-Maersk.

Figure 3. China export destinations and U.S. import origins for sea-based trade.

- The northeast economic zone would mainly develop heavy industry, machinery, raw materials, and manufacturing, as well as become the national agriculture base.
- The northern coastal zone would focus on high technology and manufacturing.
- The eastern coastal zone would be headed by Shanghai and would be developed into a comprehensive manufacturing center, becoming the most competitive region.
- The southern coastal zone would develop an outbound economy and a consumer commodity base.
- The mid-Yellow River zone would be developed into a coal, energy, iron, and steel production zone.
- The mid-Yangtze River zone would primarily develop planting and agriculture, with secondary emphasis on iron, steel, and automobile industries.
- The southwest zone would be built into a heavy industrial, textile, and tourist zone.

- The northwest zone would mainly develop energy, farm and raise livestock, and the tourist industry.

An important characteristic of this economic structure is that much of China's economic production and growth originates in the coastal provinces. For example, 93 percent of China's exports originate in these provinces. Almost 40 percent of the exports originate in the Pearl River Delta region alone (the region including Hong Kong, Shenzhen, and Guangzhou), the first region opened to foreign economic development. The Yangtze River region (Shanghai) was the second region to experience substantial economic growth. Over the past 10 years, the government has attempted to spur economic growth in the north-east and northern coastal zones, and most recently it has adopted a national investment and economic policy to support economic progress in the inland western provinces. This "Go West" policy has important implications to trade and logistics because goods manufactured in the western provinces will have to make their way to the ports on the coast, possibly increasing logistics costs.

> "China will have the infrastructure in place to handle increasing trade flows. The real problem is in Europe and the United States, where governments do not seem able or willing to invest in the transportation system. The Chinese clearly see the relationship between economic development and transportation system productivity. It is not clear if European and American officials understand this linkage."
>
> – Moller-Maersk Representative

The growth in China's GDP and its place in the global market are even more impressive when one considers the costs of logistics on the Chinese mainland. Logistics costs represent more than 20 percent of the total cost of product manufacturing and delivery (compared to around 10 percent for the United States). Many of the shippers and retailers that participated in scan meetings pointed to reducing this level of logistics costs as being the greatest productivity improvement that could occur in the Chinese market.

Caution should be exercised in interpreting the 20 percent logistics cost. In many ways, this larger percentage (compared to the United States or Japan) can be explained by the different structure of the economy. Services, which generate little freight movement, are only 32 percent of China's GDP, compared to 81 percent in the United States and 68 percent in Japan. In addition, the average value of Chinese manufactures is well below the corresponding values in the United States and Japan. Thus, it might not be surprising that China's logistics costs are a larger part of the delivered price of manufactured goods. According to a long-time economist who has observed China's economic progress for many years, "As its wage levels rise, China will need to move up the value chain, gradually reducing the ratio of transport to final prices and hence its logistics-to-GDP ratio... It is wrong to use this ratio at this time to allege that logistics services are—across the board, anyway—high cost."

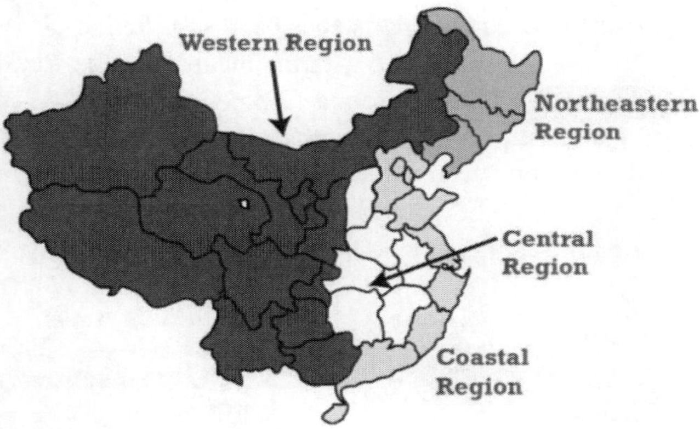

Figure 4. The four economic regions of China.

SECTION 3: CHINA'S TRANSPORTATION SYSTEM AND PLANS FOR THE FUTURE

Chinese officials at all levels of government and in the private sector agree that investing in the transportation system is one of the country's most important investment priorities. Not only does a reliable and efficient transportation system support economic development, but it also provides mobility for an increasingly mobile Chinese population.

Figure 5 shows the level of investment that has occurred since 2000 in different elements of the transportation system and the expected level of investment up to 2010, in U.S. dollars. Figure 6 shows the extent of four transportation networks in terms of network expansion.

The investment strategy in each modal network is very different, including who is involved, what type of investment is being contemplated, and the expected role each modal network is to play in the overall transportation system. Each modal network will be discussed in the following sections.

Highways

Of all the transportation investments made in China over the past 5 years, the largest amount has been dedicated to the nation's road network. In fact, the pace of investment has been so fast over the past 5 years that any comparison with years before this does not provide a good picture of what is happening with road investment today. Table 3 presents some of the most important characteristics of China's road network. As the table shows, the growth rate in both network expansion and network use has been substantial.

According to the Ministry of Communications, the total highway investment in 2006 was US$84.3 billion, a 13.6 percent increase over the 2005 investment level. Domestic loans (from the China Development Bank) and self-finance bonding accounted for the bulk of the revenue for this investment program, 40.7 percent and 32.8 percent, respectively, of the funding. Only 1.5 percent of the capital investment came from the national government budget.

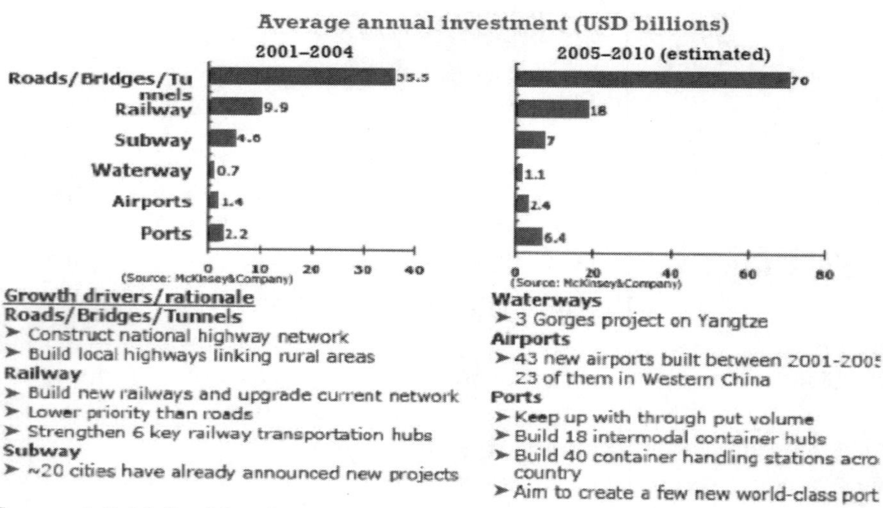

Source: A.P. Moller-Maersk.

Figure 5. Average annual total investment in Chinese transportation infrastructure (US$).

The government has plans to expand the national expressway system, as shown in figure 7. By 2010, the expressway system is expected to be 65,000 km (40,389 mi) long; by 2025, the total expressway network is expected to be 85,000 km (52,800 mi). This expressway network is designed to have seven major expressways radiating out of Beijing, nine north-south expressways, and 18 east-west expressways (the so-called 7-9-18 plan). This network is intended to link most cities with a population of more than 500,000. In addition, expressway extensions into the western provinces are aimed at increasing economic opportunity in this part of the country.

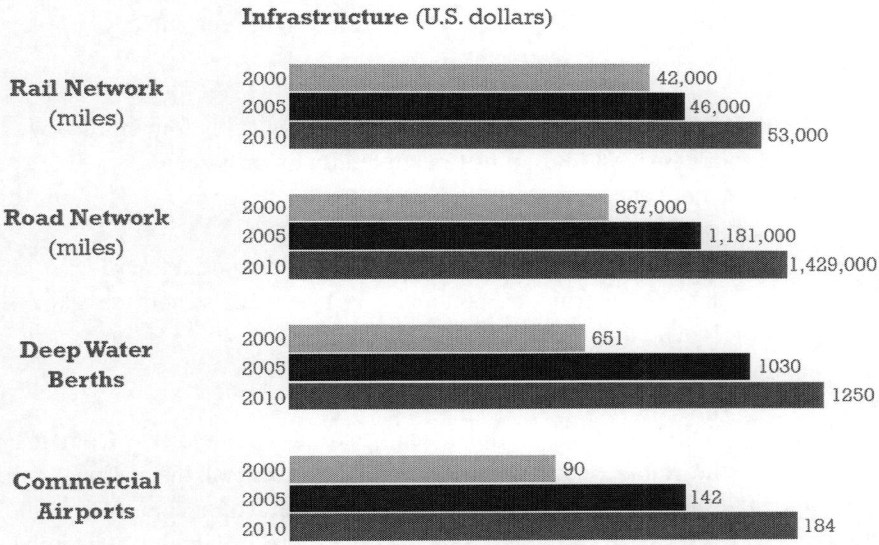

Source: APL, Inc.

Figure 6. Growth and expected growth in Chinese transportation infrastructure.

To a large extent, this expressway network is modeled after the U.S. Interstate network, with similar geometric designs and operational characteristics. Also similar to U.S. expressways, the urban portions of this network are severely congested during peak periods.

Transportation officials and U.S. shippers pointed to overweight trucks as one of the most important challenges facing Chinese transportation agencies. Given that the trucking industry consists primarily of numerous one- to three-truck firms, many markets are highly competitive. In addition, Chinese manufacturers have the right to choose the carrier for the first move from the plant, which provides a strong incentive to load a truck as much as possible to maximize revenue. The national, provincial, and municipal governments have established enforcement programs, but the sense among transportation officials is that a large number of oversized and overweight trucks are still on the road.

Rail

Chinese officials realize that the rail network needs to be improved if it is to play an important role in international trade. Figure 8 shows the major rail lines in China. Similar to the national expressway network, China plans to add to this network to create an 84,973-km (52,800-mi) main rail network by 2010 and a 100,000-km (62,137-mi) network by 2025. The current 5-year plan targeted the following rail investments:

- Build an express passenger transport network with four north-south and four east-west lines, plus three intercity express routes.
- Enhance rail access to ports.
- Target rail investments in the western region.
- Optimize rail network by electrifying and building dual track.
- Construct 18 intermodal container rail terminals and develop a double-stack container transportation route.
- Construct five major hubs.

Container movements by rail face several challenges. Container movement on the rail network carries about 2.2 percent of the national rail freight tonnage and 1.5 percent of the total container volume moved in the country. Three types of rail intermodal services are available: scheduled, unscheduled, and block trains. Scheduled and unscheduled trains have the least priority on the rail network, with military, passenger, coal, and foodstuffs coming first (the rail network is shared by freight and passenger rail services). Freight movements by rail are often unreliable and, in many markets, face stiff competition from trucking firms. Few ports have dockside rail access, so some form of intermodal transfer must occur before containers reach the port that enables them to be loaded onto a ship.

Table 3. Characteristics of China's road network, 2005–2006

Characteristic	2005	2006	% change
Total road mileage (miles)	2,078,603	2,148,080	3.3
Expressway (miles)	25,479	28,172	10.6
Freight tonnage by highway (100 million tons)	134.2	146.6	9.3
Freight ton-miles (100 million ton-miles)	5,401	6,061	12.2
TEUs carried by truck	24,649.224	35,178,263	42.7

Source: Ministry of communications, Transport Statistics Yearbook, 2006.

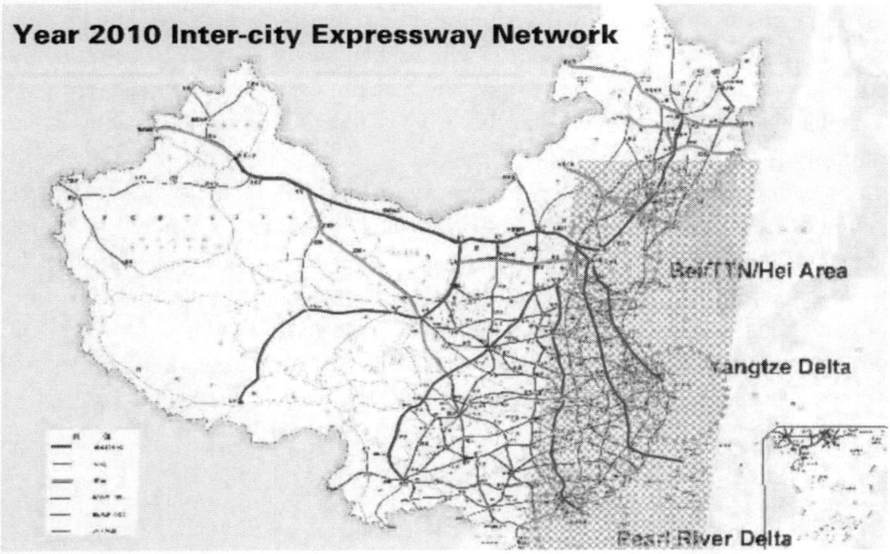

Figure 7. China's major highway network.

Figure 8. China's rail network.

China plans to invest in the freight rail network with expectations that more freight (especially containers) will be hauled by rail. A 10 million 20-foot equivalent unit (TEU) target via rail has been established as part of the 5-year planning process. Given that the level is now 3 million TEUs, this is an ambitious goal. Eighteen new intermodal yards are part of the strategy to attract more container traffic to rail. Several of these yards are open and others are under construction. New freight-only track is being constructed in major origin-destination corridors and investments are being made in rolling stock. However, unlike many of the major road projects, private investors have not actively sought investment opportunities in the rail network. Government solicitations to participate in some of the intermodal rail yard projects, for example, did not attract much attention from the investment community.

Navigable Waterways

Throughout China's history, rivers and coastal shipping routes have been major thoroughfares for commerce. The Pearl and Yangtze Rivers, in particular, have served as the commercial arteries for much of China's economic development. As noted earlier, the Pearl River Delta was the first region to experience large-scale foreign investment, becoming a major manufacturing and transportation hub of China's international trade.

Table 4 shows statistics on the importance of China's navigable water network. These statistics are national and thus hide the more local nature of barge transportation. For example, about 30 percent of the transshipments that occur in Shanghai involve barges. In the Pearl River Delta, the percentage is slightly higher. The exact percentage in the Pearl River Delta is hard to estimate because many transshipments occur in midstream from one barge to another to avoid terminal fees. Also, some terminals have limited barge access because of capacity constraints, so barges must have a minimum of six containers to berth pier-side.

Those interviewed for the scanning study had different opinions about the Pearl and Yangtze River barge operations. The sense was that too much barge capacity exists in the Yangtze River market and, given the numerous small operators (similar to the trucking industry), it is a highly competitive market. In some cases, the freight forwarder is also the barge operator, which results in a mixing of interests on expediting the movement of the container. Few berths are available for barges along the river and at the mainland port itself (this is not true for the new port built off the coast). In addition, the recent opening of a new port in Shanghai (Yangshan) many miles from the old port and located in deep water raises questions about the seaworthiness of the existing barge fleet to serve the new port.

Table 4. Characteristics of China's navigable water network

Characteristic	2005	2006	% change
Total navigable mileage (miles)	—	76,639	—
Inland river berths	—	30,942	—
Coastal port berths	4,298	4,511	5.0
Number of barges	41,000	37,000	-9.8
Fleet net dead weight (million tons)	11.0	12.0	9.0
Tonnage by waterway (billion tons)	2.2	2.5	13.2
• River	1.05	1.2	9.8
• Coastal	0.65	0.8	19.5
• Oceangoing	0.49	0.5	12.1
Ton-miles (100 million ton-miles)	30,865	34,477	11.7
• River	1,632	1,880	15.2
• Coastal	5,279	6,141	16.3
• Oceangoing	23,954	26,456	10.4
TEUs carried by water	19,400,000	23,300,000	20.21

Source: Ministry of communications, Transport Statistics Yearbook, 2006.

Table 5. Comparative costs and time to transport a TEU to Shanghai from Chongqing

Chongqing to Shanghai	Distance (Miles)	Transit Time (Days)	Cost (US$, 20-ft container)
Road	1,300	3–4 (40 hours)	$1,500
Rail	1,600	7–10	$ 540
Barge	1,500	8 (11 upriver)	$ 315

Source: APL, Inc.

For the Pearl River, the sense was that barge capacity is sufficient to handle market demand, although competition is still quite high, in this case among larger barge companies. New river ports have been constructed in the Pearl River to cater to barge traffic, thus providing more convenient intermodal transfer (although a large percentage of the transshipments occur midstream).

Table 5 indicates why inland water transportation is so important for the supply chain in China. This table shows estimated costs and transit time to move a 20-foot container from Chongqing to Shanghai, a distance of 2,092 to 2,575 km (1,300 to 1,600 mi), depending on the modal network (see map in figure 8 for the location of Chongqing). Although barge transport takes a longer transit time than truck, it costs almost 80 percent less. For commodities that are not time sensitive, barge transportation is clearly the preferred mode on the basis of cost.

Ports

The economic growth that China has experienced over the past two decades has been driven primarily by international trade. This trade could not have occurred without port capacity to handle the ever-increasing flow of containers coming from mainland factories. Figure 9 shows TEU movement for selected Chinese ports in 2006 and that expected in 2011. Growth in these ports has averaged greater than 20 percent per annum over the past 5 years, so the forecasted volumes do not appear unreasonable. Figure 10 shows a comparison between TEU throughput in Chinese and U.S. ports. Figure 11 shows the expected growth in China container movements as a share of the global market, from a 31 percent share in 2006 to an expected 34 percent share by 2011. Ten of the top 30 container ports are located in China, as are three of the top four (Hong Kong, Shenzhen, and Shanghai). By 2010, eight of the top 15 container ports will be in China, with Shanghai expected to be the largest container port in the world. The ports in Shanghai, in particular, play a significant role both in the Chinese economy and the global market. Tonnage through the ports in Shanghai will exceed 350 million in 2007, making it the largest port in the world from the perspective of tonnage moved. Shanghai has already overtaken Hong Kong as the largest container port in China (an expected 27 million TEUs in 2007), and expected future growth will only solidify this position. The new Shanghai Port of Yangshan is an example of the type of investment the Chinese are making in port infrastructure (see figures 12 and 13. The first two phases of the US$14.5 billion Yangshan deep-sea port are now open, with a 2020 target year for achieving the full capacity of the port (33 to 50 deep-sea berths) at 25 million TEUs per year. The port is located about 32 km (20 miles) offshore and is connected to the mainland by a highway bridge (there is no direct rail connection to the port, although there is a new intermodal rail yard on the mainland near the bridge gateway).

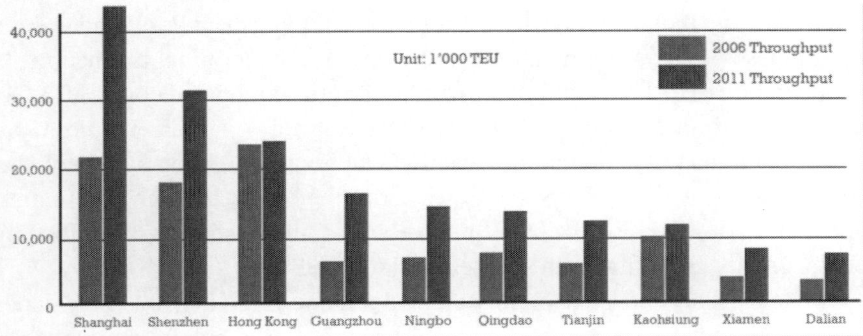

Source: A.P. Moller-Maersk.

Figure 9. TEU throughput in selected Chinese ports, 2006 and 2011.

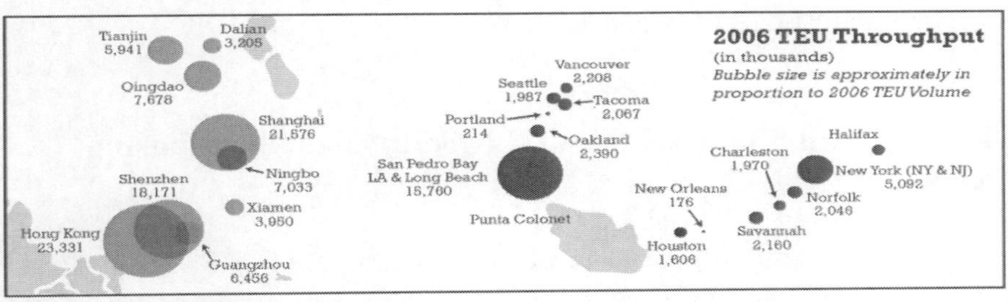

Source: A.P. Moller-Maersk.

Figure 10. TEU throughput in Chinese and U.S. ports, 2006.

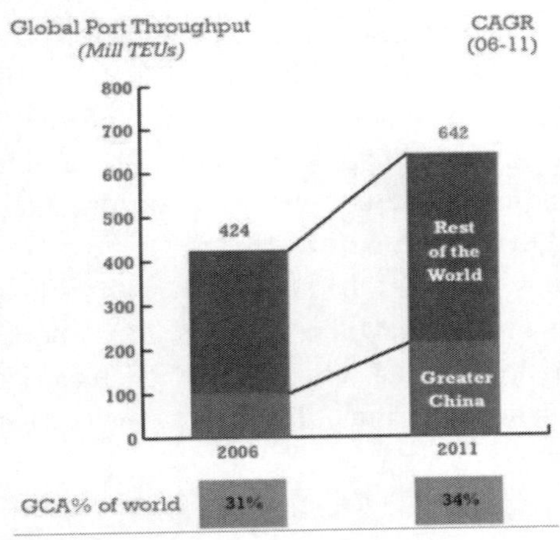

Source: A.P. Moller-Maersk.

Figure 11. Expected Chinese share of global container market.

One of the most impressive aspects of the Yangshan Port, and indeed other Chinese ports, is its operational productivity. The terminal can handle 35 TEU operations per hour per crane, with a daily throughput record of 23,044 TEUs. The terminal is open 7 days a week, 365 days a year. The terminal operator commits to loading and unloading a barge within 5 hours and a vessel within 20 hours, and it has a posted truck turn time of a maximum 30 minutes. Some ports can use seven cranes per vessel in the loading and unloading process, greatly speeding up the vessel turnaround time.

The Yangshan Port has not only created a modern facility to export goods to the world, but it has also spurred local growth. For example, the mainland entry to the port bridge has become a highly desirable location for logistics and warehousing centers. A new town has been created to house port employees, and what was once agricultural land is turning into manufacturing, freight consolidation, and warehousing sites.

Meetings with Shipping, Retail, Logistics, and Warehousing Firms

The scan team met with many representatives of U.S. retailers and shipping, warehousing, and consolidation firms. Many of these discussions focused on their perceptions of the performance of the U.S. transportation system as much as on the Chinese transport system. The major point the private sector participants in these meetings made is that they have every expectation that the Chinese government, along with private investors, will provide a transportation system that will meet the needs of the supply chain in China. Their concern is more with the ability of the United States and European Union to provide reliable transportation serving their own ports. Much of the discussion centered on the poor productivity of U.S. port operations compared to Chinese ports.

Several companies provided the scan team with estimates of future trade trends. Firms such as ProLogis, Moller-Maersk, and American Presidents Line made several observations that they believe characterize the current and expected market situation in China. The following is a compilation of their observations:

- World trade is expected to grow 6 to 12 percent a year over the next 5 years, and 80 percent of this trade will be carried by ships.

- Asian growth (especially in China) is key. More than 51 percent of worldwide container traffic passes through Asia. In 2001, international trade represented 79 percent of East Asian GDP, up from 50 percent in 1991.
- Although China still faces serious challenges ahead, its strong growth momentum will be maintained in the next 5 years.
- Key challenges facing China include deteriorating environmental conditions, undersupply of natural resources, asset inflation, an aging population, a social welfare system under pressure, employment demands because of accelerated urbanization, uneven income distribution, and protectionism in international trade.
- Coastal infrastructure is first class, but inland infrastructure is inadequate. The sources of China's economic growth are concentrated in coastal China, but growth in coastal China is slowing as costs rise. Linking coastal China to untapped inland markets is a key to the future.
- Rail use in mainland China's hinterland still remains the key bottleneck for the future. Rail rates over long distances are still challenged by truck, which enjoys fuel price protection on diesel (to a degree). There is little enforcement of over-the-road weight limit, allowing one truck to carry what would normally require two to three. This makes some long-haul truck routes competitive with rail, especially because of speed.
- Mainland China is dominated by mom-and-pop truck operators. The average trucking company has one to two trucks.
- Current ship orders (3.15 million TEUs) represent more than 45 percent of worldwide capacity. Thirty- five ships are in service with a capacity in excess of 7,500 TEUs, with orders for 126 additional ships of this size or larger.
- In North America, there is a clear trend by shippers to diversify inbound shipments to multiple ports. The goal is to minimize the risk of disruption in the supply chain in the event a single port is impacted by labor unrest, terrorism, etc.
- North American and European transportation systems are a concern because of insufficient investment in infrastructure, limited terminal capacity, road congestion, and the inability of government to provide timely investments. Harbor depths, port terminal size and equipment, capacity of regional highway and intermodal rail infrastructure, land

availability, and labor and environmental constraints will limit or enhance port growth in North America and Europe.

- Few U.S. ports will be able to accommodate post-Panamax ships, trade routes will become more concentrated between major ports, inland ports will grow in number, and interest in intermodal rail links will increase in Europe and North America. Gateway ports with good intermodal rail links to inland ports (Seattle, Houston, Rotterdam, Hamburg) may experience less warehouse demand as many containers are transported directly inland.
- The number of transshipment hubs will grow. Twenty-eight percent of the worldwide volume of containers (85 million TEUs) are transshipped. In China, new direct shipment ports are emerging in areas that traditionally used transshipment hubs. As a result, the ports at Los Angeles-Long Beach and New York-New Jersey will likely lose market share to several emerging North American ports, yet the sheer volume of containers handled at the major North American ports will remain dominant.
- Larger, multimarket, global terminal operators continue to grow (Hutchinson, Eurogate, PSA Corp., HHLA, CSX World Terminals, International Container Terminal Services, Inc.). Major shipping lines (A.P. Moeller-Maersk, Evergreen, APL, COSCO, NYK, Mediterranean Shipping Co., P&O) continue to integrate vertically, offering more value-added services (consolidation and deconsolidation, rail shuttles, logistics, third-party logistics services (3PLs), etc.). Increasingly, 3PLs and ship lines will be customers for port-related properties.
- The need for deconsolidation ware- house facilities will increase in North America and Europe, especially at the emerging direct shipment ports. Logistics providers (shipping lines and 3PLs) are increasingly seeking deconsolidation warehouse facilities where inbound product can be unloaded, mixed, and repacked for direct distribution. Proximity to port terminals is essential and foreign trade zone designation is increasingly meaningful.
- In China, facilities for import- and export-oriented activities will increase: export consolidated forwarding services for consolidation (nonbonded), international logistics (bonded), and inbound consolidated forwarding services for deconsolidation (bonded). The provision of such facilities should not be difficult, given the access to world finance markets that Chinese development projects enjoy.

Figure 12. Many container transshipments in the Pearl River basin take place in midstream, primarily to avoid fees for land terminal use.

Figure 13. The new Yangshan deep-sea port in Shanghai.

Figure 14. The new bridge connecting the Port of Yangshan to the mainland.

PORT OF QINGDAO

The city and Port of Qingdao, located in the province of Shandung on the Yellow River, has been one of the fastest growing economic centers in China. GDP growth in the province has averaged just over 16 percent a year for the past 3 years, with growth in foreign direct investment averaging just over 13 percent a year. The Port of Qingdao has been one of the fastest growing ports in China. Port officials expected about 9 million TEUs to move through the port in 2007. The United States has the highest number of container exports (19 percent), but Japan (18 percent) and South Korea (14 percent) are just behind. The European Union represents 17 percent of port exports.

Figure 15. The Port of Qingdao is one of the most efficient ports in China.

The port used to be located in center city, some 80 km (50 mi) away. However, because of community concerns about port expansion so close to neighborhoods, government officials decided that a new port should be constructed some distance away. A toll road was built to connect to the new port. Qingdao is one of six cities in China that has been given planning authority by the central government, so it has been able to develop an economic development strategy that emphasizes the competitive advantages of the surrounding region.

The port itself is one of most modern in China. It has on-dock rail facilities (one of the few in China that does), as well as barge transshipment terminals. The major terminal in the port, the QQCT terminal, is a joint venture of four shareholders—a government corporation (31 percent share), Dubai Ports (29 percent), Maersk (20 percent), and Cosco Pacific (20 percent). Just over US$880 million has been invested in the terminal to date. Terminal operations include the monitoring of key performance measures, such as gross crane rate (36.6 moves per hour), gross vessel rate (69 hours), net crane rate (40.8 moves per hour), and truck turnaround time (34 minutes).

Many other private company participants echoed the observations made by these three companies. Economic growth is expected to continue at high rates. The Chinese government is investing heavily in transportation infrastructure and is slowly opening the transport sector to foreign investment. There are areas of concern for the Chinese transportation system (e.g., the freight rail network), but generally most believed that transportation to and from the ports will not be a big issue in the future, although lowering the cost of logistics will be a major focus of both public and private organizations.

ProLogis Metrics for Evaluating Port Markets for Future China Investment

The most important criterion for investment is that a port is in the government's plan for expansion and improvement. Once this prerequisite is satisfied, the following criteria are important:

- Proximity to large local population base
- Physical port capacity for growth in TEUs handled
- Good road infrastructure
- Inland ports—intermodal rail-river connections
- For export markets, proximity to diverse manufacturing centers (e.g., Shanghai)
- Availability and cost of labor
- Frequency and availability of dedicated ocean carrier service

DEVELOPMENT OF DISTRIBUTION CENTERS: CASE OF PROLOGIS

ProLogis is the world's largest owner, manager, and developer of distribution facilities, with 44.9 million square meters (483 million square feet) of industrial space in 105 markets across north America, Asia, and Europe. The company leases its industrial facilities to 4,700 customers, including manufacturers, retailers, transportation companies, third-party logistics providers, and other enterprises with large-scale distribution needs. Since going public in 1994, ProLogis has experienced extraordinary growth. It has gone from $400 million in assets under management in just nine U.S. States to a global portfolio of properties valued at more than $34 billion. ProLogis continues to follow its customers into new markets and to extend its position as the global leader in industrial real estate.

Figure 16. The new Lingang industrial park has the road and sewer infrastructure built, waiting for development to occur.

ProLogis identified China as a major market several years ago and now has facilities in 19 markets in the country. ProLogis has also been a major player in developing the Lingang industrial park near the new Yangshan Port. The Lingang industrial area is expected to be about 300 square km (116 square mi) in area (half the size of Singapore), with land uses targeted for manufacturing, heavy industry, high tech, logistics, and residential and commercial activities. The 2020 population is expected to reach 800,000.

The ProLogis facility in Lingang, a joint venture with a state-owned agency, has an area of about 2.8 square km (1.1 square mi) and currently has 15 acres of warehousing floorspace and just over 52 acres for a container yard.

At build out, this facility is expected to have about 1.4 million square meters (15 million square feet) of usable space.

Investment in the ProLogis facility was based on expectations that the new Yangshan Port will generate large demands for both bonded and nonbonded warehousing and container-handling facilities. The local government invested in the local road infrastructure with the expectation that development would occur at some future point.

SECTION 4: GENERAL OBSERVATIONS AND LESSONS FOR THE UNITED STATES

The major observations from this scan are organized in four categories—China's economic growth and driving forces; transportation infrastructure development; governmental structure, decisionmaking, and analysis; and global shipper and carrier perceptions.

China's Economic Growth and Driving Forces

The following are observations on factors and driving forces that have contributed to China's impressive economic growth:

1. The economic growth of China over the past 10 years has been dramatic. Both **government officials and private sector representatives the team met with during the scan expected this growth to continue in the foreseeable future at or near its current rate.** The estimate for 2007 was that China's GDP would increase by about 10 percent. This follows a trend line that shows annual GDP growth of 10.4 percent per year for the past 10 years. The growth in the economy was mirrored by the office expansion of the global companies the team met with during the scan, such as the rapid expansion of subsidiary offices of APL, Maersk, and ProLogis throughout China.
2. Much of the economic growth has been fueled by private investment. **As different sectors of the economy have been opened to foreign investment, joint ventures and other financial partnerships have provided the institutional framework for the expansion of the**

economy. This is especially true in the transport and logistics sectors, where foreign investments have occurred.

3. **The economic expansion of China started in the south (Pearl River Delta), moved north based on national economic policy, and is now pushing west based on government policy.** Ninety percent of China's exports are manufactured in the coastal provinces, which is causing large demographic shifts that are straining China's resources and social fabric. The "Go West" campaign, an attempt to mitigate these strains, was a continuing theme of the team's discussions with both government officials and private sector representatives during the scan. ("West" refers to the next set of provinces west of the coastal provinces). This national campaign has significant implications to supply chain logistics costs and to the efficiency of the Chinese transportation system in moving exports to the coastal ports. With logistics costs already high in China (about 20 percent of GDP), the movement of manufacturing westward will require efficient intermodal services leading to the coastal ports, 643 to 804 km (400 to 500 mi) away.
4. Although China has had large urban populations for centuries, urbanization has reached unprecedented levels over the past 10 years. Much of China's economic expansion has occurred in urban areas, where the large population provides a substantial labor force. However, many laborers move from one urban area to another looking for jobs, so large portions of the urban labor force are transient. **The consequence of such large urban concentrations is that the central government must pay particular attention to these populations and provide resources to make sure their basic needs are met.** The term "social harmony" was an often-heard theme to describe the intent of governmental programs. **From a transportation perspective, the consequence of this policy focus is that passenger transportation often receives priority over freight movement (although in port cities freight movement often receives close attention from transportation officials).**
5. Environmental degradation and energy consumption are consequences of China's rapid economic growth and the equally rapid increase in its urban populations. Air quality in particular has received increased government attention. **Although it appears that economic development is still the primary goal of governmental policy, additional goals and performance measures relating to**

environmental quality and energy consumption have been added to the national agenda.

Transportation Infrastructure Development and Operations

The following are observations on the characteristics of China's transportation infrastructure and how it has been provided:

1. **Recognizing the vital role that transportation plays in its goal of continued economic growth, China is investing heavily in transport infrastructure, over 9 percent of the country's GDP. This investment comes from both public and private (joint venture) sources.** The current 5-year plan has allocated billions of dollars for a national expressway system, new freight rail lines, port improvements, and 18 new rail intermodal yards. Much of the national investment in transportation is intended to attract private investment to specific facilities, such as toll roads.
2. **Substantial levels of private capital are being invested, in some cases with low expectations of rapid return on investment,** but investors anticipate long-term benefits from investing in China. This investment has occurred primarily over the past several years in highways, port facilities, and logistics parks. Private investment has been sought in rail infrastructure and intermodal terminals with limited success.
3. **China is leveraging its natural geography to facilitate movement of goods. River and coastal shipping continues to be a significant component of China's intermodal transportation system.** The Pearl and Yangtze Rivers traditionally have been China's highways to the world. To a large extent, this is true today. China relies on barges and coastal shipping to access its major ports served by rivers. For example, about 40 percent of the containers shipped to Shanghai's new Yangshan Port arrive by barge. New barge-only ports upstream of the Pearl River Delta provide a similar percentage of barge traffic to several container ports in the delta. The central government is also adopting barge design and energy standards along with subsidies for their adoption to improve consistency and efficiency in barge operations. For the development of the ports along the Bohai Bay, rail and truck access is used to bring cargo to the port facilities.

4. **The central government's "Go West" policy has shifted investment attention to inland transportation and the challenges facing such transportation, especially the connections to the major international ports.** In cases where barge transportation can be used cost-effectively, such as on the Pearl and Yangtze Rivers, inland economic development relies on barge transportation to move a large percentage of the intermodal freight. However, where barge transportation is not feasible or economical, government investment in highway and rail networks provides alternative means of accessing the coast. Both the trucking and barge industries, however, are highly fragmented and consist of many small owner-operators, offering few of the economies of scale that occur with larger companies. Although the market for moving containers is competitive, the limited capacity of individual barge and trucking firms forces shippers to deal with many different operators, increasing the transaction costs associated with moving substantial levels of intermodal freight to the coast.
5. **China's intermodal rail service faces significant challenges.** The movement of containers receives low priority on China's rail network, following military, passenger, energy (i.e., coal), and food movements. Accordingly, intermodal rail movement tends to be unreliable, often with no scheduled departures. It is estimated that rail handles about 2 percent of the intermodal moves in the country. However, the government is investing heavily in improving this service. Eighteen intermodal yards are in various stages of development, although those that are open are lightly used because of network reliability problems. About 12,000 km (7,456 mi) of freight-only track are being built to separate passenger and freight movements. A goal of 10 million TEUs carried by rail (now less than 3 million) has been established for the current 5-year plan period. However, even with a threefold increase in TEUs handled (which will be a challenge), the market share for rail intermodal movements will still be only 3 percent.
6. **The Chinese central government has encouraged joint ventures to finance the national expressway system, stretching government funds to support a variety of new modal investments.** Historically, tolls on these expressways have not been used to influence travel behavior, but to raise revenue. **However, consideration is now being given in some locales to using tolls to influence truck movement.** In Shanghai, for example, a distance-based toll system on a ring road

was converted to a considerably less expensive flat toll rate to encourage trucks accessing the port to use the ring road and reduce congestion on other inner-city expressways. This is exactly what happened, but this mechanism is not always possible. The three tunnels between Kowloon and Hong Kong are tolled. The ability to change toll rates is limited, so the older tunnel, priced lower than the other two, has considerably more traffic and is routinely congested. Governmental authorities face heavy resistance to toll increases for social reasons, so the other two toll tunnels, even though they provide what could be viewed as premium service for a higher price, are underused.

Chinese toll rates are comparable to those in the United States and Europe, but the Chinese believe this does not reflect the economic reality of travelers in China, where the per capita GDP is much lower. Accordingly, the Chinese are trying in some cases to renegotiate concession agreements to allow lower toll rates, but offset lower toll revenues with longer concession time periods (from 30 to 50 years).

There was some limited indication that, as in the United States, the tolling of highways can run into public opposition. In Hong Kong, for example, truckers and the public opposed tolls on a new highway, so the government had to use its own funds rather than private investment to build the road. The official in charge noted that this represented a perspective of a road as a social asset rather than an economic one.

7. **The national expressway plan is centered primarily on three major economic and political centers: Beijing, Shanghai, and the Pearl River Delta.** In essence, the national expressway system will be the major means of connection between the political and economic centers of the country, reinforcing their importance in the economic future of China. The scan team noted that all of the new intermodal rail terminals are next to a national expressway, as are ports and major airports. **Intermodal connection has been an important consideration in network design.**
8. **Trucking is the predominant means of moving containers to and from the ports, especially in the river delta manufacturing regions.** The trucking industry consists mainly of small businesses (one to three trucks), which makes its contribution to China's economic growth even more impressive. No standard vehicle configuration exists, and little integration of technology in trucking

operations is apparent. Truck movements respond to changes in cost structure, as the Shanghai example above shows. The trucking industry is maturing, with a variety of strategies being used or considered to improve industry productivity. Different strategies are being considered for different purposes. American trucking companies are entering into partnerships with Chinese companies to provide financial capital and expertise.

The makeup of the Chinese trucking industry also means that containers do not move considerably beyond the port facilities. Goods are brought into consolidation-deconsolidation facilities, where they are placed in containers for export or devanned for further movement inland. It will be interesting to see how these operations change as China's trucking industry matures and commercial motor vehicles more closely resemble those in the United States or European Union, as well as when China's intermodal rail network is complete and containers can be loaded directly onto double-stack rail for movement west.

9. **Given the relatively large number of trucking businesses in China and the intense competition for freight movements, the team was not surprised to find that oversized and overweight trucks have become an important concern to transportation officials.** Chinese officials are developing a national strategy for enforcing size and weight regulations, especially on the country's new expressway system, and are considering fixed truck weigh stations. They apparently are not seriously considering weigh-in-motion technologies. A national campaign to enforce load limits has been in place for about a year.
10. **Chinese port productivity is the best in the world.** Chinese ports operate 24 hours a day, 7 days a week, 365 days per year. Operational strategies are impressive—cranes that lift four TEUs, 20- to 30-minute truck turns, nine cranes working one ship, etc. New ports are being developed and the capacity of existing ports is being expanded rapidly. Although the scan team did not examine any safety data, terminal operators noted that the safety record for Chinese terminals was as good as, if not better than, terminals elsewhere in the world.
11. **Given the significant level of trade to the United States and current U.S. legislation, security compliance was a growing concern for port terminal operators.** The relatively new infrastructure at China's ports allows terminal operators to build

security measures into terminal operations, especially using technologies screening outbound containers. One terminal in Hong Kong has undertaken a 3-year demonstration to show how X-ray and other scanning technologies can be used to screen all containers entering the terminal with minimal disruption to terminal efficiency.

12. **China has not progressed to the point of systematically managing its infrastructure; it is still in the "build" mode.** Nevertheless, at a few of the more mature areas experiencing significant congestion transportation officials indicated a need to begin paying serious attention to system management.
13. **Intermodal connectivity and landside access to Chinese ports are not approached differently or in a more sophisticated way than in the United States or European Union.** With the exception of a truck-only access road that was retrofitted from the national network to the Port of Yantian, there was little evidence of the Chinese building into their large container port facilities a dedicated capacity to maintain free flow of cargo. The general consensus is that the congestion would be dealt with when it arrived.
14. **Rail access to maritime port facilities is not being consistently built into new port design.** With the exception of the Port of Qingdao, which has no river access and which is being looked at as the entry port for land bridge cargo from the rest of Asia to the European Union and Russia, no other port facility was being built with on-dock rail. This appears to reflect the lack of reliability that stems from the low priority intermodal cargo has on the rail network (fourth behind passengers, energy, and agricultural products) and that the majority of the goods made for export are manufactured in the coastal provinces, making the distance from manufacturing facility to export port less than 500 km (310 mi). How this will play out with the building of the 18 intermodal rail terminals and the "Go West" policy will be interesting to watch.

Governmental Structure, Decisionmaking, and Analysis

The following are observations on the institutional structure and process of making transportation investment decisions in China:

1. **China's policymaking and implementation process identifies national goals, some of which have performance metrics. However, local officials have leeway in implementing projects so that they also meet local objectives.** A national 5-year plan provides policy direction on what will be emphasized during the plan's timeframe (China is now in its 11th 5-year plan).
2. The transportation agencies in the national government have different responsibilities focusing on different modes (e.g., Ministry of Communications, Ministry of Railways, Ministry of Construction). **Because governmental officials' performance is measured by results, they pay attention to measures of progress. National data are collected and analyzed on overall modal performance and the state of the economy.** Some challenges the national transportation agencies face are responsible for the sometimes conflicting roles of planning, operating, and regulating a modal system. Some viewed this as a hindrance to achieving progress on performance goals. This was the specific reason the CRCT was separated from the Ministry of Railroads and given the sole responsibility of operating the rail network.
3. **Data analysis is used to determine the extent to which goals are being met at different levels of government.** Some referred to this as "results-oriented planning." The port terminals are all private operations and the terminal operators routinely use metrics.
4. **The performance of local officials and local governments is measured against national goals.** Many noted, for example, that the most important metric for local officials is the degree to which economic growth occurs during their tenure, defined primarily as job growth for residents. China's tax policy also supports this goal, because the tax revenue from the economic activity in a province stays, for the most part, in the province. Local officials clearly understand the linkage between expanding transportation infrastructure and their ability to create new economic development. While economic development is still the primary metric and motivator, growing environmental concerns appear to be increasing attention on measuring governmental performance on environmental quality (for example, the number of days cities experience a certain level of air pollution).

5. Although the scan team did not conduct a systematic assessment of the capability of municipal government agencies to plan and provide for transportation infrastructure and services, every meeting with local officials included the staff members responsible for each mode. In other words, **all of the modes were located in one agency, which encouraged the adoption of a multimodal systems perspective when looking at regional transportation investment.** For example, in Shenzhen the relationship among sea cargo, barge transportation, highway travel, and air cargo was discussed with an understanding of how each affected the other. The same was true in the other municipalities visited.
6. **In most cases, there was little evidence that Chinese officials sought advice from carriers or shippers on national strategic transportation plans or investments. However, at the provincial and regional levels the inclusion of the private sector in tactical investment decisions was evident in the number of public-private partnerships.** Although not reflective of the common practice on the mainland, in Hong Kong, an advisory committee to the government consisting of carriers and shippers routinely provides advice on overall transportation policy. Also, the national government is seeking advice from the private sector as the 18 intermodal rail hubs are being developed.
7. **Port development plans considered modal access strategies as part of the planning process, but it did not always result in multimodal port access.** The officials responsible for ports, and especially newer ports, were very aware of and concerned about port access. Planning for ports included attention to highway and barge access and, in the case of Shenzhen, rail. This represented a much broader, multimodal perspective on planning than is usually found in the United States. Rail access to the ports is limited, primarily because of a perception that the rest of the intermodal rail network suffers from unreliable and slow service.
8. **Project development occurs much faster in China than in the United States.** Transportation projects are viewed as a priority for economic development, so they move forward rapidly. Chinese officials noted that project alignments and other project characteristics were sometimes modified by environmental considerations, but they could not identify any project that was stopped for environmental reasons. Given the rapid growth in China's economy and the need for

expeditious provision of supporting infrastructure, it is not surprising that environmental considerations are not viewed as a controlling factor in project development (similar to the early years of the U.S. Interstate Highway System). However, it appears that environmental considerations are becoming more important to local officials and that future project development efforts will be influenced even more by such factors.

9. **In keeping with the national policy of social harmony, government officials are concerned about the negative impact of transportation facility operations and expansion on local communities.** For example, there was evidence that at least two new ports that replaced central city ports were built some distance from the city center to reduce traffic and development pressures on the surrounding communities and the complications of inner-city congestion. When community displacement does occur, efforts are made to mitigate the impacts (e.g., a new logistics park that displaced farmers trained them to earn a living in the logistics park).
10. **Hong Kong's role in the competitive market of the Pearl River Delta is evolving.** Having the largest container port terminals in south China positioned Hong Kong as a major port of departure for mainland exports. However, new ports in nearby Shenzhen and along the Pearl River (along with dredging in the river to allow access to these ports for bigger ships), as well as new manufacturing development on the west bank of the river, will likely cause a shift in container exports to other ports. Second, certain cost advantages associated with exports through Hong Kong could soon disappear because of infrastructure improvements on the mainland. Third, containers can enter Hong Kong only on trucks driven by Hong Kong drivers. This labor cost is much higher than comparable movements to the Shenzhen ports. Once the special tariffs expire, the cost structure for goods moving though Hong Kong's terminals will not be very advantageous. It remains to be seen how the market will adjust to these changing conditions, but it appears that Hong Kong's relative position in global container flows could evolve in a different direction in the future.

Shipper and Carrier Perceptions

The following are observations made by shippers and carriers in the China market:

1. **Many of the international ocean carriers and shippers the team met with during this scan view the serious constraint in international trade and supply chain efficiency as being on the receiving end, in Europe and the United States.** The prevalent perception is that terminal through-put in the United States and European Union is limited by terminal operational limitations, landside access capacity, and growing road congestion. There was a strong perception that the United States lacks the political will to invest in infrastructure and could not deliver needed investments in infrastructure in a timely manner even if desired. China is viewed as proactive on infrastructure provision by building for the future and clearly stating in its strategic plans what will be built and when. The United States, on the other hand, is perceived as reactive. The biggest complaint was the length of time it took to reach decisions on transportation projects. Industry representatives expressed an understanding of governmental laws, regulations, and structures, but were frustrated with not knowing a project's fate for a long period of time, so long in some cases that other investment or logistics decisions could not be made.
2. **Shippers and carriers believed that the effect of a widened Panama Canal and increased transits through the Suez Canal will likely be more shipments heading to east coast ports, but that west coast ports will still be the major destination for most containers.** The shifting of sea routes is in response to transportation costs and the reliability of ground access modes at the west coast ports. With increased capacity at the Panama Canal, some carriers believed it would become a more appealing route than rail or truck services across the continental United States. In addition, carriers mentioned that one constraint in all movements is that the new generation of container ships (10,000 to 12,000 TEUs) cannot physically dock at most U.S. ports. The larger ships are used primarily to serve Europe because of market factors and the capacity of many European ports to handle larger vessels.

3. Several shippers and carriers said bunching of vessel departures from Chinese ports (because of when merchandise arrives at the ports and when it is needed in the U.S. market) causes a significant peaking problem. They observed that a peaking in departures from China usually results in a peaking in arrivals at U.S. ports, especially Los Angeles-Long Beach. **Several shippers and carriers believed that this peaking phenomenon could be remedied by working with retailers, shippers, and manufacturers.**

Lessons for the United States

The lessons learned from this scan are organized in two major categories—consequences to the United States and its transportation system, and different approaches to planning and project development in support of a growing economy.

Consequences to the United States and the U.S. Transportation System

1. Under current economic projections in the United States and China, trade flows from China to the United States will continue to grow. China is building the infrastructure to handle them, but there are questions about whether the U.S. transportation system is ready. With a limited number of ports of entry, the U.S. transportation system necessarily concentrates these imports at a few strategic locations. **For the United States to remain competitive globally, investment in transportation infrastructure is needed, new system management technologies should be applied, and institutional change in how the country identifies, funds, operates, and makes targeted infrastructure improvements to key elements of the national transportation system should be considered.** These improvements help not only to expedite the movement of imported goods, but also to reduce the logistics cost of U.S. companies to compete in the global market.
2. **Trade from China increasingly will become an east coast issue.** With new service routes through the Suez and Panama Canals, States on the east coast will experience increasing demands on their transportation systems. Shippers and carriers noted that these routes will become even more important if land access to west coast ports deteriorates.

3. Given the navigable draft and terminal capacity of most U.S. ports, **the largest container ships will not provide service to the United States.** This means that U.S. ports will be served by vessels carrying less than or equal to 10,000 TEUs. With increasing cargo volumes, that means more vessel calls.
4. **Similar to what scan teams observed during the intermodal freight scans in Europe and Latin America, the team noted a dramatic difference in port efficiency between China and the United States.** Hours of operation, the time to turn trucks, crane productivity, and good land access make Chinese ports very efficient. If U.S. ports are unable to physically expand because of community concerns or terrain limitations, maximizing the use of existing capacity and improving port throughput are imperative to the United States' ability to handle increasing container flows.
5. **The United States can learn much from China on using natural geography to the maximum extent, particularly in the use of barge and coastal shipping as access modes to major ports.** In China, the Pearl and Yangtze River ports are being developed as transshipment ports, and new manufacturing capacity is being developed and located to take advantage of river transport. Although the United States has few locations where manufacturing concentration is along navigable rivers that connect to major ports, the Chinese experience in barge operations might be informative in those locations where such operations make sense. Even if U.S. river systems and the ports they serve do not provide logical conduits for containerized freight movement, they provide key assets for bulk commodity movement. They need to be well maintained to ensure that goods move efficiently and do not shift to an already-burdened rail and highway network.
6. **Freight bottlenecks are viewed as a drain on transportation system and economic productivity.** This is a perspective the United States should adopt as well. Solving these bottlenecks involves more than just expanding physical capacity. It also involves using technology and operational strategies. The Port of Yantian is a good example. Ten years after the port was built, it became apparent to local officials that congestion on the roads serving the port was affecting not only freight movement, but also local traffic. They built a truck-separated access route to the port to eliminate the bottleneck.

7. **Chinese officials recognize that freight-oriented transportation investments, especially near ports, are an important part of the nation's economic development. Accordingly, Chinese transportation agencies have implemented system management strategies aimed at improving port access.** Efforts to encourage more efficient movement of trucks have included setting differential tolls, prohibiting trucks in congested areas, enhancing enforcement of pedestrian and passenger vehicle flows on streets near ports, separating trucks from passenger highway lanes, and encouraging the use of barges as an alternative access mode (although rail does not appear to be a major consideration at this point).
8. **The United States is fortunate to have a much more developed rail network, which in many cases provides on-dock service to port terminals. This is a significant advantage to U.S. trade flows and one that needs to be nurtured.** The efficiency of the feeder services into and out of U.S. ports will be a key factor in the ability of the U.S. transportation system to support increased container demands from China. The U.S. rail network, although facing congestion issues of its own, still provides an indispensable capacity for moving containers once they reach U.S. ports. Improving the productivity of such services will be an important element of the U.S. strategy to remain competitive in the global market. The team noted that the new Chinese freight-only rail track being built to connect the 18 new intermodal hubs will have no at-grade crossings.
9. **Given China's experience with oversize and overweight vehicles and the infrastructure damage it is grappling with, the United States should ensure that its commercial motor vehicle size and weight program continues to advance and receive adequate resources.** This is a critical part of the road management system. As the scan team learned in China, when such a program is not in place, roads wear out much faster than expected. Thus, Federal and State efforts to monitor and enforce appropriate size and weight standards on the Nation's road network need to be continued and supported.
10. **One challenge facing west coast ports is the bunching of vessel departures from China that result in vessels arriving at about the same time in the United States.** This is primarily due to operations in which ships depart Chinese ports over the weekend in response to manufacturing, supply chain, and market requirements. If vessel bunching could be reduced, this could significantly benefit both U.S.

and Chinese ports. Shippers and carriers in China expressed some optimism that this could in fact occur.

How the Chinese Invest In and Operate Their Transportation System to Support a Growing Economy

1. **China has a national transportation investment policy that is closely linked to its trade and economic policy.** It was clear in discussions with Chinese officials at all levels of government that they were aware of the national transportation policy and what it is intended to accomplish and supported it. **China competes as a nation.** National transportation investment appeared to focus on two major goals (besides military defense): strategies to foster social harmony among Chinese citizens and strategies to support economic growth, with the second goal supporting the first. Given where China is in its development cycle, there is little question that **transportation infrastructure is considered a critical component of the nation's economic future** and that creating a transportation infrastructure network is critical to and in some cases leading the economic development pattern. The United States would benefit from adopting national transportation investment policy that supports the nation's economic health and global competitiveness. Transportation, trade, and economic policies that coordinate transportation investment, especially freight-related investment, are vital.
2. The Chinese central planning function is not a model that would work in the United States. However, **it is worth considering a strategic investment plan for the national expressway network that is financially supported at the national level and executed locally (similar to the initial effort to build the U.S. Interstate Highway System) and that uses performance measures to monitor progress in developing and operating key system elements.** A centrally planned and financially supported national expressway network provides the platform for China to compete as a nation—a united whole that works for the benefit of the entire nation. The three-tiered planning effort the Chinese employ—which covers central, provincial, and local needs—appears to work well in addressing national, intraregional, and local transportation needs. For example, performance measures and standards for the Interstate Highway System might be established nationally, with the means of achieving desired performance left to the States.

3. Many assets that work in tandem with the Chinese transportation system (port terminal development, logistics parks, etc.) are funded through private investment. In some cases, it may take years for the investment to start producing net gains. However, companies made it clear they are willing to invest in China because the Chinese can make decisions and show progress toward infrastructure improvement. A similar confidence in the U.S. approach to decisionmaking and project development was lacking. For instance, a number of private sector representatives pointed to the length of time it takes to complete the environmental process on U.S. projects. They noted that it often exceeds the time companies can place a planned project or investment on hold. While they did not indicate that the United States should stop mitigating environmental impacts, they did point out that a more streamlined process for environmental (or other public) decisions could allow the private sector to look more favorably on business and capital investments. Companies know that in China they will get a timely decision on a proposed investment, but they have little confidence in the U.S. process for assuring that progress will be made. **This suggests that if the United States is interested in fostering economic development and encouraging more private investment in transportation facilities, it needs to place greater emphasis on timely public sector decisionmaking. Agencies simply need to get to the decision point earlier.**
4. The joint venture is the primary instrument of privatization in China. **In almost all cases, private investors do not get a majority share of the investment (the exception being port terminals); government agencies or state-owned enterprises retain control.** In some instances, such as the development of 18 intermodal rail yards, private investors have turned down participation in a joint venture because the government stipulations were too stringent. The major lesson, however, is that the model of private funding in China is that government participates in a significant way by steering where the investments can be made.
5. **Chinese planning for intermodal centers and indeed for regional transportation networks adopts a systems perspective on performance and investment.** The regional highway network, ports, airports, intermodal facilities, and ware-housing and distribution centers appear to be planned with an understanding of how they interconnect and affect one another. While multistate coalitions seek

to coordinate multijurisdictional activity in the United States, more effort along these lines will be necessary to achieve systems-level coordination.

6. The team learned that Hong Kong's international airport has been the busiest airport in the world since 1996 for international air cargo—not because of air cargo planes, but because of the freight shipped as belly cargo in passenger aircraft. The air cargo market in Hong Kong has grown rapidly but is not viewed as a new market, given the long-established air cargo business in Hong Kong (with the United States as the single largest destination for air cargo originating in Hong Kong). **Air cargo is the fastest growing segment of freight movement. While it still is only a small percentage of total tonnage, the implication to the U.S. transportation system of this growth in both air cargo hubs and belly freight is new stress to the transportation network on already-stressed and overcrowded U.S. airports.**
7. National data collection in China provides a springboard for national transportation planning, investment, and performance evaluation. This is especially true for investment in freight facilities and services. This is an important lesson for the United States. **U.S. freight data systems should not only be continued, but expanded to provide the information needed for optimal transportation investment decisionmaking, especially given the important role that freight plays in the Nation's economic health.**

SECTION 5: IMPLEMENTATION STRATEGIES AND RECOMMENDATIONS

The scan team developed the following preliminary recommendations for activities that should follow from the scan:

1. The results of this scan are a wakeup call on the need for the United States to invest in transportation infrastructure with a more national perspective if it is to stay competitive in a global market. This first, and perhaps most important, recommendation is to revive a national focus for U.S. transportation officials. This effort would focus on the

importance of the transportation-economic integration so evident in China. Key messages in this effort include the following:

- Federal, State, and local governments cannot dismiss the potential lessons to be learned from the Chinese experience because of preconceived notions that China's form of governance has no application in the United States. Major differences in governance exist between the two countries, but that should not preclude U.S. consideration of successful concepts being deployed in China, such as unified national goals and performance measures. Similar concepts were once a vital part of U.S. initiatives such as the building of the Interstate Highway System.
- Transportation policy with a national perspective needs to be integrated with other key national and State-level policies. This integration could relate to economic development, trade, community development, environmental quality, etc.
- Transportation investment should be targeted to those elements of the national system that meet the established policy goals. Performance measures should be established and monitored to gauge the level of success achieved.
- A national transportation policy has room for both public and private sector roles and responsibilities. China is ahead of the United States in the use of private investment in the transportation sector. In an era when resources are limited, private investment opportunities should be provided throughout the transportation system.

2. A study of the Yantian Port truck highway facility should be commissioned. This case study would be conducted by the Chinese Academy of Transportation Systems. It would focus on the metrics the Chinese used to quantify the congestion they experienced, how they used those metrics to vet potential solutions, and how they determined that a dedicated truck lane was the most appropriate solution. The study would also cover how, if at all, the Chinese have documented the effect of the new access road on the congestion they sought to resolve.
3. The Chinese governance structure uses established performance measures and national data collection extensively to manage transportation policy. The scan team believes this approach has useful constructs, but it is unclear what specific measures China uses. The concept of establishing performance goals or levels for national

systems (such as the U.S. Interstate Highway System) has a potentially useful application in the United States. A study should be undertaken to understand how the Chinese government develops and uses performance measures to manage its national transportation policy. In the long term, it would be interesting to compare and contrast the available performance measures of both countries.

4. A major observation of the scan was the need for a better understanding of the scheduling and operation of ship movements to the U.S. west coast. Because of long-standing traditions and market considerations, most ships leave China during the weekend and arrive on the U.S. west coast at about the same time, placing peak demands on port operations. It became clear during the scan visit that opportunities exist to work with retailers, manufacturers, logistics providers, shippers, carriers, and terminal operators to flatten out this peak arrival distribution. FHWA will conduct a preliminary analysis of vessel bunching to develop a better understanding of the nature of vessel arrival times in key U.S. ports. If the data show that a problem does exist, FHWA will convene a forum to address the streamlining of vessel bunching at U.S. ports.
5. This report is the third of three that have documented international scans on intermodal freight and connectivity in different parts of the world. The scan team recommends that a synthesis be undertaken of all three scan findings to determine what has been learned, the implications to the United States of these lessons, and the research and training opportunities that should be developed on these topics to educate the U.S. transportation community.
6. China appears to have a wealth of data on freight, ports, etc., that is of interest to the U.S. transportation community. It would be beneficial to both countries to compare national data collection strategies and to share information of mutual benefit. The U.S. Department of Transportation should pursue a data exchange program between FHWA and the U.S. Research and Innovative Technology Administration and the Chinese Ministry of Communications. A memorandum of understanding (MOU) has been signed, so the scan team's recommendation is to implement this MOU as soon as possible.
7. Chinese officials expressed an interest in learning how the U.S. truck information management system works. A comparison should be made between U.S and Chinese truck information management

systems to see if there are areas of joint benefit and possible applications in the United States.

8. The Chinese are in the early stages of truck size and weight enforcement strategies. They are starting to recognize the damage that overweight vehicles cause on the road network. FHWA should make information available to relevant Chinese agencies on size and weight enforcement methodologies, including weigh-in-motion technologies, and identify possible further technology exchange opportunities.
9. The scan team has identified numerous conferences and meetings at which the results of this scan could be presented. Scan team members will pursue as many of these opportunities as possible. Other outreach efforts will target specific audiences, such as congressional committees, national commissions, Federal and State agencies, and professional organizations.
10. Much of what was reported from this scan reflects the poor level of understanding that elected officials and the general public have of China and its emerging role as a trade super- power. Educational and public outreach efforts should be undertaken to inform key constituencies. This would include incorporating the results of this scan (and the other two freight scans) into professional training courses, especially those focused on freight movement.
11. Given the rapid pace in economic growth and the corresponding expansion of the transportation system, consideration should be given to visiting China again in a few years to see what has happened in several key areas. Among the questions that it would be useful to explore are the following:
    - How might the further development of rail in China affect passenger and freight movement?
    - What lessons can the United States learn as it invests in its rail system?
    - What has been the impact of private investment on transportation facilities?
    - How have new security technologies been incorporated into port terminal operations?
    - What has been the impact of the "Go West" campaign on logistics costs?
    - To what extent are barges still an important mode of access to coastal ports?

- How has the massive investment in port and inland transportation infrastructure affected the relative competitive advantage of different Chinese ports?
- How has the trucking industry evolved in vehicle technology and industry structure?

APPENDIX A: SCAN TEAM MEMBERS

Contact Information

David Cole ***(AASHTO Cochair)***
Commissioner, Maine Department of Transportation
16 State House Station Transportation Building Augusta, ME 04333
Telephone: (207) 624-3003
Fax: (207) 624-3001
E-mail: david.a.cole@maine.gov

Tony Furst ***(FHWA Cochair)***
Director, Office of Freight Management
FHWA, HOFM-1
1200 New Jersey Ave. SE Washington, DC 20590
Telephone: (202) 366-2201
Fax: (202) 366-3225
E-mail: tony.furst@dot.gov

Sharon Daboin
Deputy Secretary for Performance Improvement
Governor's Budget Office
7th Floor Verizon Tower
303 Walnut Street
Harrisburg, PA 17105-3441
Telephone: (717) 787-2033
Fax: (717) 787-0827
E-mail: sdaboin@state.pa.us
Warren Hoemann
Senior Vice President–Industry Affairs
American Trucking Associations
950 North Glebe Road, Suite 210

Arlington, VA 22203-4181
Telephone: (703) 838-7956
Fax: (703) 838-1781
E-mail: whoemann@trucking.org

Dr. Michael D. Meyer *(Report Facilitator)*
School of Civil & Environmental Engineering
Georgia Institute of Technology
790 Atlantic Dr. Atlanta, GA 30332
Telephone: (404) 385-2246
Fax: (404) 894-2278
E-mail: mmeyer@ce.gatech.edu

Richard Nordahl
Chief, Office of Goods Movement
California Department of Transportation
Division of Transportation Planning, MS 32
PO Box 942874
Sacramento, CA 94274-0001
Telephone: (916) 653-0426
Fax: (916) 653-1447
E-mail: richard.nordahl@dot.ca.gov

Marygrace Parker
Freight Mobility, Safety, and Security Program Coordinator
I-95 Corridor Coalition
3206 Tower Oaks Blvd. Rockville, MD 20852
Telephone: (518) 436-2817
Fax: (518) 692-8640
E-mail: i95mgp@ttlc.net

Leo Penne
Program Director
Intermodal & Industry Activities
AASHTO
444 North Capitol St. NW, Suite 249
Washington, DC 2001
Telephone: (202) 624-5813

Fax: (202) 624-5806
E-mail: lpenne@aashto.org

Norman Stoner
Division Administrator
FHWA Illinois Division
3250 Executive Park Dr.
Springfield, IL 62703
Telephone: (217) 492-4730
Fax: (217) 492-4230 or 4621
E-mail: norman.stoner@dot.gov

Dr. Tianjia Tang
Office of Freight Management, Room 6320
FHWA
1200 New Jersey Ave. SE Washington, DC 20590
Telephone: (202) 366-2217
Fax: (202) 366-3225
E-mail: tianjia.tang@dot.gov

Biographic Sketches

David Cole (AASHTO cochair) is the commissioner for the Maine Department of Transportation. He is responsible for planning, building, and maintaining Maine's transportation system, including highways, bridges, mass transit, rail-roads, ferries, ports, airports, and bicycle and pedestrian trails. Before his appointment as commissioner, Cole served as president and chief executive officer of the Eastern Maine Development Corp., focusing on entrepreneurial development and advocacy at the local, State, and national levels, including reverse foreign investments. Cole also became a member of the Maine Port Authority in 1997. Cole serves on the Board of Directors of the American Association of State Highway and Transportation Officials (AASHTO) and is vice chair of the AASHTO Subcommittee on Intermodal Transportation and Economic Development. Cole graduated from the University of Maine and with a master's degree in public administration.

Tony Furst (FHWA cochair) is a senior executive with the Federal Highway Administration (FHWA) in Washington, DC. Furst is director of the Office of Freight Management and Operations, which develops freight policy for FHWA, provides data analysis and decision-support tools for transportation professionals evaluating freight projects, develops and promulgates professional capacity-building programs and training for freight professionals, provides truck size and weight program guidance and interpretation, and evaluates and promotes freight technology development for national and international deployment. Before joining FHWA, Furst held a range of positions in the U.S. Department of Transportation, including program coordinator with the Maritime Administration, regional coordinator for intermodal projects in the Northeastern States and California in the Secretary of Transportation's Office of Intermodal-ism, and branch chief of the Maritime Infrastructure Security Branch in the Maritime and Land Security Directorate of the Transportation Security Administration. Furst is a retired U.S. Coast Guard officer. He has a bachelor's degree in marine biology from Florida State University and a master's degree in business administration from the University of Washington.

Sharon Daboin was the deputy secretary for aviation, rail freight, ports, and waterways for the Pennsylvania Department of Transportation (PennDOT) when this scan took place. She oversaw the administration of financial assistance grants and technical assistance to more than 135 public-use aviation facilities and 67 regional and shortline railroad operators. Daboin was PennDOT's lead on intermodalism, participating in multimodal, multistate transportation studies and initiatives. Daboin represented PennDOT on the Aviation and Rail Freight Advisory Committees, cochaired the Delaware Valley Regional Planning Commissions' Goods Movement Task Force and the Pennsylvania Air Service Committee, and was a member of the AASHTO Standing Committees on Aviation and Rail Transportation (cochairing the task force for State programs), the I-95 Corridor Coalition, and the South Central Pennsylvania Regional Goods Movement Steering Committee. Before joining PennDOT, Daboin held several positions in the Federal Aviation Administration, including manager of the Harrisburg Airports District Office. Daboin served 4 years in the U.S. Air Force and has a bachelor's degree in organizational management from Pennsylvania's Eastern University.

Warren E. Hoemann is a senior vice president with the American Trucking Associations (ATA). Hoemann oversees ATA councils and conferences and is the ATA liaison with key affiliate organizations. Before joining ATA in 2006, Hoemann was deputy administrator of the Federal Motor Carrier Safety Administration at the U.S. Department of Transportation. Before his Federal government service began in 2003, Hoemann had a long career in the trucking industry. He was vice president of the California Trucking Association and vice president of government relations for Yellow Corporation (now YRC Worldwide), where he handled the company's political and legislative affairs in the 50 States and U.S. Congress. From 1978 to 1986, Hoemann was the general counsel for the Western Highway Institute, a nonprofit trucking industry research organization. He started his career as a private attorney in Denver, CO, representing motor carriers. Hoemann is a Phi Beta Kappa graduate of St. Olaf College in Minnesota with a law degree from the University of Colorado School of Law. He has studied international law at Cambridge University in England and has spoken at universities on trucking issues.

Dr. Michael D. Meyer (report facilitator) is a professor of civil engineering in the School of Civil and Environmental Engineering at the Georgia Institute of Technology. He is also director of the Georgia Transportation Institute. Meyer has conducted research on transportation investment planning and program development, systems engineering, and intermodal transportation. Before joining Georgia Tech, he was director of transportation planning and development for Massachusetts, and before that he was a professor of civil engineering at the Massachusetts Institute of Technology (MIT). Meyer has published more than 180 articles on topics related to transportation decisionmaking and has served on numerous national transportation committees. He is a graduate of the University of Wisconsin-Madison and holds a master's degree in civil engineering from Northwestern University and a Ph.D. in civil engineering from MIT. He is a licensed professional engineer in Georgia and served as chair of the Executive Committee of the Transportation Research Board in 2006.

Richard Nordahl is chief of the Office of Goods Movement at the California Department of Transportation. His office, part of the Division of Transportation Planning, is responsible for statewide goods movement planning, including the analysis of goods movement by truck and rail and movement through California's airports, seaports, and border crossings. His responsibilities include developing major portions of the Goods Movement Action Plan of the California Business, Transportation, and Housing Agency and the California Environmental Protection Agency. His foreign experience includes participation in the U.S.-China Modern Logistics Conference in Beijing in May 2004 and an October 2006 briefing of China Ministry of Communication officials. Other major assignments include serving as the department's acting chief of planning in San Diego, staff to Gov. Gray Davis' Commission on Building for the 21st Century, and project manager and assistant project manager for the 1993 California Transportation Plan. Nordahl holds a degree in environmental studies from California State University and a certificate in rail transportation from the University of California's Institute for Transportation Studies.

Marygrace M. Parker serves as program coordinator for freight mobility, safety, and security for the I-95 Corridor Coalition, an alliance of transportation and related agencies in the 16 States from Maine to Florida. Parker provides program oversight and coordination for the coalition's Intermodal Freight and Commercial Vehicle Operations program committees. She oversees a number of coalition studies, including assessment of rail operational bottlenecks in the Northeast, Mid-Atlantic, and Southeast I-95 Corridor regions and the potential for short sea shipping along the I-95 Corridor/Eastern Seaboard. Before joining the coalition staff, she served as director of the Office of Traffic Management for the New York State Thruway Authority, where she oversaw the various bureaus responsible for traffic operations, communications, emergency management, and intelligent transportation systems. Parker is a former New York State Police officer. She holds a bachelors' degree in criminal science from Russell Sage College. She has served on several technical committees for the Transportation Research Board and National Cooperative Highway Research Program panels.

R. Leo Penne is program director for intermodal and industry activities with the American Association of State Highway and Transportation Officials (AASHTO). He is responsible for issues involving freight transportation by all modes—rail, truck, aviation, ports, and waterways—and for liaison with industries with significant interests in freight movement. He shares responsibility for developing and communicating the case for the economic benefits of transportation and for demonstrating the linkage between transportation and economic development. Penne has initiated and carried out programs for advocacy, policy development, and research in areas such as transportation, economic development, urban development, environmental protection, public finance, training, and tourism and has written and edited books, reports, and articles on these subjects. He has held positions dealing with issues of strategy and policy analysis for the State of Nevada, the U.S. Department of Commerce, and the National League of Cities. He holds degrees in political science from Seattle University and the University of Washington and has served as an adjunct faculty member at the University of Maryland.

Norman R. Stoner is the administrator for the FHWA Illinois Division. He leads the Illinois Division's professional staff in partnership with State and local highway agencies to deliver an effective Federal-aid highway program in Illinois. Stoner has been active in the Chicago Region Environmental and Transportation Efficiency Program (CREATE), an effort to relieve rail freight and highway congestion in the Chicago freight hub. Since joining FHWA in 1969, Stoner has served in a variety of positions and in other FHWA offices, including the Michigan Division, where he was involved in projects addressing growing freight demands at the border crossing with Canada. Stoner received his bachelor's degree in civil engineering from Ohio University and is a registered professional engineer in Ohio.

Dr. Tianjia Tang is a transportation specialist for FHWA in Washington, DC. He is responsible for the Freight Analysis Framework (FAF) and the Freight Modeling Improvement Program (FMIP). The FAF provides strategic analysis of commodity movements in the United States related to transportation infrastructure and investment needs. It supports policymaking and legislation development and enactment. The FMIP is developing a new generation of freight forecasting and modeling tools for State and local government agencies to use in transportation planning, programming, and project development processes. Before joining FHWA's headquarters staff in 2004, Tang served as highway engineer and environmental specialist in FHWA's Resource Center in Atlanta, GA, and Baltimore, MD. Before his Federal tenure, he served in a wide range of positions, including project engineer, project manager, and megaproject development and design manager with a State DOT and private consulting firms. Tang is a Ph.D. graduate of the University of Arkansas and a registered professional engineer in Georgia. He is a member of the American Society of Civil Engineers and serves on several freight-related technical committees of the Transportation Research Board.

APPENDIX B: AMPLIFYING QUESTIONS

The following questions indicate the type of information that the U.S. delegation is interested in obtaining during our visit. We have organized the questions from the perspective of the professional responsibilities of the individuals we would like to talk to. In addition, we have listed primary questions, or questions we want to focus on during our visit, and secondary questions, or questions we would like to discuss if time permits or to obtain answers from other sources.

National Transportation Policy Officials

Primary Questions

1. Please briefly describe the relationship among the central government, provincial government, local government, and private freight operators as it relates to the movement of freight. Who owns and operates what part of the nation's freight transportation system? What does the national government regulate with respect to freight transportation (for example, vehicle requirements, pricing, etc.)? What is expected to be funded and operated by the government? By private companies?
2. Is there a national freight policy on transportation's role in economic development, mobility, and system investment? If so, what are the specific elements of this policy that relate to international trade and investment in the nation's transportation system? What does the policy say about the relative role and investment in harbors and seaports, railroads, highways, and inland water infrastructure? How are national decisions made on which mode or intermodal facilities will receive investment (for example, investing in highway versus rail, or one port versus another)? In what agency are these decisions made? Who is involved? How does the government provide for an integrated transport system in its decisionmaking process?
3. What are the most important economic and transportation factors influencing transportation system investment decisions? What performance measures are considered when making investment decisions (for example, reduce travel time, increase travel time reliability, reduce transportation cost, and create new jobs and economic opportunity in underserved parts of China)? Do you collect data on the performance of China's transportation system? If so, what data are collected?
4. How does China's transportation system accommodate freight and passenger traffic? Do they use the same infrastructure? Which takes priority in investment and operations? How is the decision made to invest in one type of transportation project (for example, for passenger movement) versus another that will provide greater benefit to freight movement?
5. How are trade and transportation policy coordinated? How is China's national transportation policy linked to a national energy policy, and what role does the freight sector play in this relationship?

6. To what extent are public-private partnerships and partnering agreements used to fund transportation infrastructure, particularly with financial equity arrangements? To what extent is private sector input included in determining what transportation investments are made?
7. What are the most challenging issues China faces on the movement of freight? What do you think will be the most challenging issues in the future (for example, 10 years from now)?
8. How are environmental considerations (for example, air quality and water quality) addressed when transportation investments are made? Similarly, how are community concerns (for example, urban development and land use) addressed when such investments are made?

Secondary Questions

1. Is there a widespread understanding of the importance of freight transportation and support for major freight infrastructure projects at all levels of government?
2. From a pricing standpoint, how competitive is truck compared with rail and river transport? Does the government play a role in determining these prices or is the market deregulated?
3. When investments are made, do the calculations provide estimates of the cost to maintain in the future?
4. What other factors (such as the 2008 Summer Olympics in Beijing) are driving the nation's transportation policy and investment strategies?
5. So that you may best export goods to U.S. customers, what changes in U.S. infrastructure would you like to see occur? What level of Chinese investment in U.S. transportation infrastructure do you foresee?
6. Are certain revenue sources dedicated exclusively to transportation at the national, provincial, or local levels? If so, please describe. Does the national government have a dedicated capital budget for major transportation investments or are investments by the government treated as part of the general budget?

National Transportation Planning and Engineering Officials

Primary Questions

1. For China's highway network:
   - Please describe China's national highway investment plan. What steps are being taken to improve China's road network (for example, new highways serving major ports)?
   - Do you separate local and passenger traffic from freight traffic to and from your ports?
   - Have you or are you planning to develop lanes or highways dedicated exclusively to truck traffic? If so, are they for port connectors, bypasses to urban congestion, or longer segments of the highway system?
   - How do you determine truck size and weight limits to protect your road infrastructure investment? How do you enforce those limits?
   - What are the key challenges facing the movement of freight by highway?
   - When investments are made, do the calculations provide estimates of the cost to maintain in the future?
2. For China's rail network:
   - Please describe China's national rail investment plan. Is there a policy to attain a certain share of freight movement by rail?
   - What steps are being taken to improve China's rail network (for example, investing in rail lines to allow double stacking of containers or separating passenger and freight rail lines)?
   - What rail investments are being made to improve rail access to your export-import ports?
   - What percentage of your total rail freight traffic is intermodal (that is, uses containers)?
   - Will your new rail lines be completely grade separated?
   - When investments are made, do the calculations provide estimates of the cost to maintain in the future?
   - What are the key challenges facing the movement of freight by rail?
3. For China's inland water system:
   - Please describe China's national inland water system investment plan. Is there a policy to attain a certain share of freight

movement by water? What steps are being taken to improve the nation's inland water network (for example, investing in inland intermodal ports or improving river navigation)? How important is your inland water system for both container and bulk freight movement in the future?

- What inland water investments are being made to improve water transport access to your export and import ports?
- Do you see coastal shipping (that is, from one Chinese port to another) as an important element of your future freight transportation system?
- When investments are made, do the calculations provide estimates of the cost to maintain in the future?
- What are the key challenges facing the movement of freight by river and canal?
- Who is responsible for maintaining navigation channels and how it is being funded?

4. How long does it take to move a major freight infrastructure investment from the original proposal to completion? What are the major planning and project development steps followed in this process?
    - How do you balance investment in access corridor versus intermodal terminal needs? Line-haul versus distribution systems? Urban versus rural regional needs?

Secondary Questions

1. Do you have a national database that describes the flow of freight on the different modes of transportation? What kind of national freight data does this database include? At what level of geographic detail do you collect data—national, provincial, local? Are data required from private operators of port terminals and other freight carriers?
2. How do you link information on port traffic to decisions on investment in landside transportation?
3. Are there opportunities for sharing data on freight traffic between the United States and China that would benefit both?
4. What types of new technologies are being considered for the movement of freight (for example, magnetically levitating (maglev) trains, innovative port handling systems, etc.)?
5. Do you use a national freight transport model to predict future freight flows? If so, what kind of modeling tool do you use?

6. To what extent are vehicles standardized in the country? For example, are all heavy trucks designed to the same standard and weight limitations? Rail cars? Barges? Do you have hours-of-service regulations for truck drivers? Do truck size and weight standards affect distribution center activity?
7. Can you provide examples in which investment has been made in the nation's freight system to minimize or eliminate the need to transfer freight from one mode of transportation to another?
8. What projections of future growth are you using for freight volumes and passenger traffic? To what degree are you separating domestic and international movements? For international trade, how are export-versus-import considerations taken into account? To what extent are your projections broken out geographically, international (global versus regional) versus domestic perspectives? How are these projections used in transportation investment decisions?

Provincial, Municipal, and Port Government Officials

Primary Questions

1. What are the most important economic and transportation factors influencing transportation system investment decisions in your jurisdiction? What performance measures are considered when making investment decisions (for example, reduce travel time, increase travel time reliability, reduce transportation cost, and create new jobs and economic opportunity in underserved parts of your jurisdiction)?
2. Do you have a policy or plan that relates to transportation's role in economic development, mobility, and transportation system investment? If so, how is freight movement included in this policy? What does the policy or plan say about the relative role and investment in harbors and seaports, railroads, highways, and inland water infrastructure? How are decisions made on which freight facilities will receive investment? How does your agency provide for an integrated transport system perspective in its decisionmaking process?
3. Is your transportation system designed to accommodate both freight and passenger traffic? Do they use the same infrastructure? Which takes priority in investment and operations? How is the decision made

to invest in one type of transportation project (for example, for passenger movement) versus another that will provide greater benefit to freight movement?

4. How are environmental considerations (for example, air quality and water quality) considered when transportation investments are made? Similarly, how are community concerns (for example, urban development and land use) considered when such investments are made? To what extent is port development integrated into the community's development plan?
5. How are provincial, municipal, and port freight transportation projects funded? To what extent are public-private partnerships and partnering agreements being used to fund transportation infrastructure, particularly with financial equity arrangements? To what extent is private sector input included in determining what transportation investments are made?
6. What are the most challenging issues your jurisdiction or government faces on the movement of freight? What do you think will be the most challenging issues in the future (for example, 10 years from now)?

Secondary Questions

1. What types of projects are you considering to improve land access to your port? For example, are you building new port access roads? New barge facilities?
2. Is there a widespread understanding of the importance of freight transportation and support for major freight infrastructure projects among officials in your jurisdiction?
3. For port officials, how do you link information on port traffic and expected movements to decisions on investment in landside transportation?
4. How long does it take to move a major freight infrastructure investment from the original proposal to completion? What are the major planning and project development steps followed in this process?

Freight Carriers, Terminal Operators, and Shippers

Primary Questions

1. Generally, what is the role of foreign investment in intermodal freight facilities? Ownership? Construction? Operations? For a new intermodal freight terminal or facility or a major expansion of an existing one, who has general responsibility for and pays for the following:
   - Planning?
   - Design and construction?
   - Operations?

   If government funds are used to support these activities, are the funds dedicated solely to that purpose?
2. What are the underlying ownership arrangements for the transportation modes that serve intermodal facilities (rail, trucking, barges, etc.)? The intermodal facility itself? The surrounding land? The individual equipment components (chassis, etc.)?
3. In the siting of freight intermodal terminals or other freight-related facilities, to what degree are national, provincial, or municipal land use planning objectives taken into account? How are projects linked to the plans and activities of surrounding communities? Similarly, how are environmental concerns addressed in building and expanding facilities? What is the process for identifying and remediating any adverse environmental and community impacts that would be produced by the facility?
4. What are the key factors that drive intermodal facility capacity design? How is freight "surge" accommodated? Has there been any consideration of using departure control strategies to minimize congestion at the port? To what extent do security concerns affect facility productivity?
5. To what extent are you included in the decision- making process on changes to landside access, both rail and highway, for the terminals you operate?
6. What expectations are you under to operate your facilities 24 hours a day, 7 days a week to maximize use of the existing infrastructure?

Secondary Questions

1. What is the transport mode split in freight moving to this facility (that is, what percentage arrives by inland water, rail, or highway)? In your

opinion, what are the key factors in the decision to access your facility by each access mode? In other words, why does some freight come by train and other by truck?

2. To what extent is freight demand being directed or modified though the application of user charges (fees or tolls)? Are such charges limited to those applied to transport carriers (for example, tolls for trucks), or are they also being imposed on users of the intermodal facility (for example, a per container fee)?
3. How would differences in labor rules and expectations, safety, and security procedures account for differences in productivity at different intermodal facilities?
4. What kind of a benefit-cost analysis is done to determine whether the facility is justified?
5. What are the major benefits associated with investment in this intermodal facility? Access to labor? Better access and handling capacity to final markets? Improved financial performance? Minimized shipper costs? Enhanced freight handling productivity?
6. What performance measures are used to monitor the performance of the intermodal facility (for example, productivity measures, delay, etc.)? How are data collected in support of these performance measures? How are reliability, travel time, throughput, cost, or environmental impacts measured and considered?
7. To what extent has automated data collection been designed into terminal operations? What freight movement or vehicle tracking capabilities are available? If there are such systems, how widely are they used?

APPENDIX C: HOST COUNTRY CONTACTS

Jens Eskelund
Director-Government Relations
Maersk China, Ltd.
China World Tower 2, 30th Floor
1 Jian Guo Men Ave.
100004 Beijing
People's Republic of China
E-mail: gcacorpmng@maersk.com

Nancy Q. Sun
CRCT
China Railway Business Plaza, Suite 723
24 Yaziqiao Road, Xuanwu District
100055 Beijing
People's Republic of China
E-mail: nancy.sun@crct.com

Juguang Li
Department of International Cooperation
Ministry of Communications
11 Jianguomennei Avenue
100736 Beijing
People's Republic of China
E-mail: lijg@moc.gov.cn

Xiaoqing Shi
Secretary-General
Qingdao City Logistics Association
Eastern Coach Station Office Building, Room 1215
33 Lishandong Road
266100 Qingdao
People's Republic of China
E-mail: shixiaoqing@qdla.org

Cecil C. C. Lee
General Manager
Qingdao Qianwan Container Terminal Co., Ltd.
Fenjin 4th Road
Port of Qianwan
Huangdao District
266500 Qingdao
People's Republic of China
E-mail: cecil.lee@qqct.com.cn

Siobhan M. Das
Director-Committees
AMCHAM Shanghai
Shanghai Centre, Suite 568

1376 Nanjing Road West
200040 Shanghai
People's Republic of China
E-mail: siobhan.das@amcham-shanghai.org

Jeffrey Bernstein
Managing Director
Emerge Logistics Co., Ltd.
PO Box 040-080
200040 Shanghai
People's Republic of China
E-mail: jeffrey_bernstein@emergelogistics.com

Michelle Liu
Director
BNSF Railway International Services
Shanghai Times Square, Unit 2903
93 Huaihai Middle Road
200021 Shanghai
People's Republic of China
E-mail: chengdong.liu@bnsf.com

William Chan
Vice President & Managing Director
APL China Co., Ltd.
9f, Raffles City Office Tower
268 Xi Zang Road Central
200001 Shanghai
People's Republic of China
E-mail: william_chan@apl.com

Samuel Michael
National Account Manager
ProLogis
Azia Center, Room 2708
1233 Lujiazui Ring Road, Pudong
200121 Shanghai
People's Republic of China
E-mail: msamuel@prologis.com

Helen Yang
Shanghai Municipal Construction & Communications Bureau
100 Da Gu Road
200003 Shanghai
People's Republic of China
E-mail: hyyang@jsw.shanghai.gov.cn

Jian Hua Zhu
Deputy Director-General
Shanghai Municipal Port Administration Bureau
13 ZhongShan East Road
200002 Shanghai
People's Republic of China
E-mail: zhujh@sse.net.cn

Charles Guowen Wang
Director-Research Center of Logistics
China Development Institute
CDI Mansion
1 Jinhu Road, Silver Lake
518029 Shenzhen
People's Republic of China
E-mail: cwang@cdi.com.cn

George Goldman
Vice President-HK and South China
APL Co. Ltd/APL Logistics
16th floor, Wharf T&T Centre
7 Canton Road, TST Kowloon
Hong Kong
E-mail: george_goldman@apl.com

Lawrence Cheung
General Manager
APL Co. Ltd/APL Logisitics
Kerry Centre, Room 2309-12
518001 Shenzhen
People's Republic of China
E-mail: lawrence_cheung@apl.com

Candy Liu
Bureau of Communications of Shenzhen Municipality
Highway Hub Management & Control Center, Zhuziling
Shennan Road, Futian
518040 Shenzhen
People's Republic of China
E-mail: herewithcandy@yahoo.com.cn

John R. Harries
Port Development Director Hutchison Ports South China Terminal 4
Container Port Road South
Kwai Chung
Hong Kong
E-mail: harries.john@hit.com.hk

Charles G. Wellins
Maersk Hong Kong Limited
Vice President-Sales, GCA
19th floor, Sunning Plaza
10 Hysan Avenue, Causeway Bay
Hong Kong
E-mail: gcasalmang@maersk.com

Frank Jensen
General Manager-Commercial
Modern Terminals
Berth One, Kwai Chung
Hong Kong
E-mail: fj@modernterminals.com

Janice Tse
Deputy Secretary (Transport)
38th floor, 2 Exchange Square Connaught Place, Central Hong Kong
E-mail: janicetse@thb.gov.hk

INTERNATIONAL TECHNOLOGY SCANNING PROGRAM

The International Technology Scanning Program, sponsored by the Federal Highway Administration (FHWA), the American Association of State Highway and Transportation Officials (AASHTO), and the National Cooperative Highway Research Program (NCHRP), evaluates innovative foreign technologies and practices that could significantly benefit U.S. highway transportation systems. This approach allows for advanced technology to be adapted and put into practice much more efficiently without spending scarce research funds to re-create advances already developed by other countries.

FHWA and AASHTO, with recommendations from NCHRP, jointly determine priority topics for teams of U.S. experts to study. Teams in the specific areas being investigated are formed and sent to countries where significant advances and innovations have been made in technology, management practices, organizational structure, program delivery, and financing. Scan teams usually include representatives from FHWA, State departments of transportation, local governments, transportation trade and research groups, the private sector, and academia.

After a scan is completed, team members evaluate findings and develop comprehensive reports, including recommendations for further research and pilot projects to verify the value of adapting innovations for U.S. use. Scan reports, as well as the results of pilot programs and research, are circulated throughout the country to State and local transportation officials and the private sector. Since 1990, about 70 international scans have been organized on topics such as pavements, bridge construction and maintenance, contracting, intermodal transport, organizational management, winter road maintenance, safety, intelligent transportation systems, planning, and policy.

The International Technology Scanning Program has resulted in significant improvements and savings in road program technologies and practices throughout the United States. In some cases, scan studies have facilitated joint research and technology-sharing projects with international counterparts, further conserving resources and advancing the state of the art. Scan studies have also exposed transportation professionals to remarkable advancements and inspired implementation of hundreds of innovations. The result: large savings of research dollars and time, as well as significant improvements in the Nation's transportation system.

In: Freight Mobility and Connectivity … ISBN: 978-1-63321-422-4
Editor: Lillian Emmett

Chapter 2

CHINA-U.S. TRADE ISSUES*

Wayne M. Morrison

SUMMARY

U.S.-China economic ties have expanded substantially over the past three decades. Total U.S.-China trade rose from $2 billion in 1979 to $562 billion in 2013. China is currently the United States' second-largest trading partner, its third-largest export market, and its biggest source of imports. China is estimated to be a $300 billion market for U.S. firms (based on U.S. exports to China and sales by U.S.-invested firms in China). Many U.S. firms view participation in China's market as critical to staying globally competitive. General Motors (GM), for example, which has invested heavily in China, sold more cars in China than in the United States each year from 2010 to 2013. In addition, U.S. imports of low-cost goods from China greatly benefit U.S. consumers, and U.S. firms that use China as the final point of assembly for their products, or use Chinese-made inputs for production in the United States, are able to lower costs. China is the largest foreign holder of U.S. Treasury securities ($1.3 trillion as of November 2013). China's purchases of U.S. government debt help keep U.S. interest rates low.

Despite growing commercial ties, the bilateral economic relationship has become increasingly complex and often fraught with tension. From the U.S.

* This is an edited, reformatted and augmented version of a Congressional Research Service publication, CRS Report for Congress, RL33536, dated February 10, 2014.

perspective, many trade tensions stem from China's incomplete transition to a free market economy. While China has significantly liberalized its economic and trade regimes over the past three decades, it continues to maintain (or has recently imposed) a number of state-directed policies that appear to distort trade and investment flows. Major areas of concern expressed by U.S. policy makers and stakeholders include China's relatively poor record of intellectual property rights (IPR) enforcement and alleged widespread cyber espionage against U.S. firms by Chinese government entities; its mixed record on implementing its World Trade Organization (WTO) obligations; its extensive use of industrial policies (such as financial support of state-owned firms, trade and investment barriers, and pressure on foreign-invested firms in China to transfer technology in exchange for market access) in order to promote the development of industries favored by the government and protect them from foreign competition; and its policies to maintain an undervalued currency. Many U.S. policy makers argue that such policies harm U.S. economic interests and have contributed to U.S. job losses. For example, one study estimated that Chinese IPR infringement cost the U.S. economy up to $240 billion annually. There are a number of views in the United States over how to more effectively address commercial disputes with China:

- Take a more aggressive stand against China, such as increasing the number of dispute settlement cases brought against China in the WTO, or threatening to impose trade sanctions against China unless it addresses policies (such as IPR theft) that hurt U.S. economic interests.
- Intensify negotiations through existing high-level bilateral dialogues, such as the U.S.-China Strategic & Economic Dialogue (S&ED), which was established to discuss long-term challenges in the relationship. In addition, seek to complete ongoing U.S. negotiations with China to reach a high-standard bilateral investment treaty (BIT), as well as to finalize negotiations in the WTO toward achieving China's accession to the Government Procurement Agreement (GPA).
- Encourage China to join the Trans-Pacific Partnership (TPP) negotiations and/or seek to negotiate a bilateral a free trade agreement (FTA) with China.
- Continue to press China to implement comprehensive economic reforms, such as diminishing the role of the state in the economy and implementing policies to boost domestic consumption.

Economic and trade reforms begun in 1979 have helped transform China into one of the world's fastest-growing economies. China's economic growth and trade liberalization, including comprehensive trade commitments made upon entering the World Trade Organization (WTO) in 2001, have led to a sharp expansion in U.S.-China commercial ties. Yet, bilateral trade relations have become increasingly strained in recent years over a number of issues, including a large and growing U.S. trade deficit with China, resistance by China to appreciate its currency to market levels, China's mixed record on implementing its WTO obligations, infringement of U.S. intellectual property (including through cyber espionage), and numerous Chinese industrial policies that appear to impose new restrictions on foreign firms or provide unfair advantages to domestic Chinese firms (such as subsidies). Several Members of Congress have called on the Obama Administration to take a tougher stance against China to induce it to eliminate trade and economic policies deemed harmful to U.S. economic interests and/or inconsistent with WTO rules. This report provides an overview of U.S.-China commercial relations, including major trade disputes.

MOST RECENT DEVELOPMENTS

On January 23, 2014, Lenovo, a Chinese technology company, announced that it would purchase IBM's x86 server business for $2.3 billion. On January 29, 2014, Lenovo announced that it would acquire Motorola Mobility from Google for $2.9 billion.

From November 9 to 12, 2013, the Communist Party of China held the 3rd Plenum of its 18th Party Congress, a meeting that many analysts anticipated would result in the initiation of extensive new economic reforms. Following the meeting, the Communist Party issued a communique with a number of broad policy statements. One highlighted by the Chinese media was that the market would now play a "decisive" role in allocating resources in the economy.

On September 26, 2013, the Chinese government announced that it would join negotiations in the WTO for a trade in services agreement.

On August 5, 2013, the USTR announced that the United States had largely prevailed in a WTO dispute settlement case against China over its use of high antidumping and countervailing duties on U.S. chicken broiler products.

On July 17, 2013, the USTR expressed disappointment over the suspension of WTO negotiations on reaching a new information technology agreement, stating that China's hardline position in the negotiations was largely to blame for lack of an agreement.

On July 10-11, 2013, the fifth round of talks under the U.S.-China Strategic and Economic Dialogue (S&ED) was held in Washington, DC. China announced its intention to negotiate a high-standard bilateral investment treaty with the United States that would include all stages of investment and all sectors.

On June 7-8, 2013, President Obama and Chinese President Xi Jinping held discussions on major bilateral issues. President Obama warned that if cyber security issues are not addressed and if there continues to be direct theft of United States property, then "this was going to be very difficult problem in the economic relationship and was going to be an inhibitor to the relationship really reaching its full potential."

On May 29, 2013, Shuanghui International Holdings, the majority owner of China's largest meat processing enterprise, announced it was seeking to purchase Smithfield Foods, the largest U.S. pork producer, for $7.1 billion. Although several Members of Congress expressed concern over how the acquisition would affect U.S. food safety, the deal was completed on September 26, 2013.

On March 11, 2013, Tom Donilon, National SecurityAdvisor to President Obama, stated in a speech that the United States and China should engage in a constructive dialogue to establish acceptable norms of behavior in cyberspace; that China should recognize the urgency and scope of the problem and the risks it poses to U.S. trade relations and the reputation to Chinese industry; and that China should take serious steps to investigate and stop cyber espionage.

On February 19, 2013, Mandiant, a U.S. information security company, issued a report documenting extensive economic cyber espionage by a Chinese unit with alleged links to the Chinese People's LiberationArmy (PLA) against 141 firms, covering 20 industries, since 2006.

U.S. TRADE WITH CHINA[1]

U.S.-China trade rose rapidly after the two nations reestablished diplomatic relations (in January 1979), signed a bilateral trade agreement (July 1979), and provided mutual most-favored-nation (MFN) treatment beginning in 1980.[2] In 1979 (when China's economic reforms began), total U.S.-China trade (exports plus imports) was $2 billion; China ranked as the United States' 23rd-largest export market and its 45th-largest source of imports. In 2013, total bilateral trade (exports plus imports) reached $562 billion. China is currently the second-largest U.S. trading partner (after Canada), the third-largest U.S. export market (after Canada and Mexico), and the largest source of U.S. imports. In recent years, China has been one of the fastest-growing U.S. export markets, and the importance of this market is expected to grow even further, given the pace of China's economic growth, and as Chinese living standards continue to improve and a sizable Chinese middle class emerges. According to one estimate, China is currently a $300 billion market for U.S. firms if U.S. exports to China and sales by U.S.-invested firms in China are counted.[3]

A major concern among some U.S. policy makers has been the size of the U.S. trade deficit with China. That deficit rose from $10 billion in 1990 to $266 billion in 2008; it fell to $227 billion in 2009 (due largely to the effects of the global economic downturn), then rose over each of the next three years, reaching $318 billion in 2013 (see Table 1 and Figure 1). For the past several years, the U.S. trade deficit with China has been significantly larger than that with any other U.S. trading partner and several trading groups. Some analysts contend that the large U.S. trade deficit is an indicator that the trade relationship is unbalanced, unfair, and damaging to the U.S. economy, while others argue that the large U.S. trade deficit with China is a reflection of global supply chains because a significant level of U.S. imports from China come from foreign-invested multi-national companies there, which use China as the final point of assembly for many of their products (discussed more fully later in the report). Ajoint study by the Organization for Economic Cooperation and Development (OECD) and the WTO estimated that the U.S trade deficit in China would be reduced by 25% (in 2009) if bilateral trade flows were measured according to the value-added that occurred in each country before it was exported.[4]

U.S. Merchandise Exports to China

U.S. merchandise exports to China in 2013 were $122 billion, up 10.3% over 2012 levels. In 2013, China was the third largest U.S. merchandise export after Canada and Mexico (see Figure 2). From 2000 to 2013, the share of total U.S. exports going to China rose from 2.1% to 7.7%. As indicated in Table 2, the top five merchandise U.S. exports to China in 2013 were oilseeds and grains; aircraft and parts; waste and scrap; motor vehicles; and navigational, measuring, electro-medical, and control instruments. As indicated in Table 3, from 2004 to 2013, U.S. exports to China increased by 349%, which was the fastest growth rate for U.S. exports among its top 10 export markets.

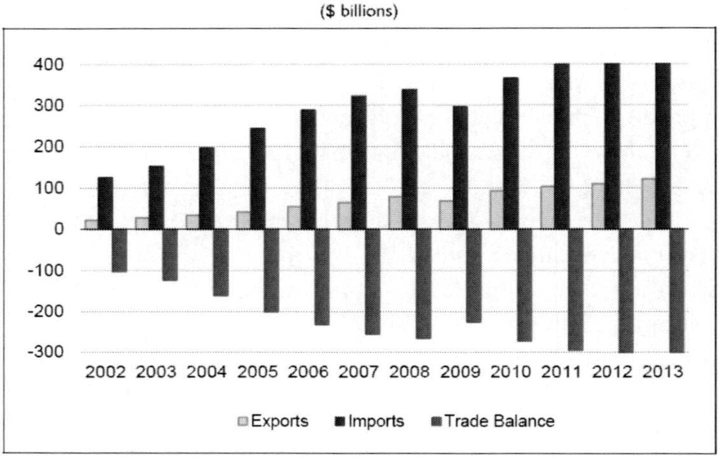

Source: U.S. International Trade Commission DataWeb.

Figure 1. U.S. Merchandise Trade with China: 2002-2013 ($ billions).

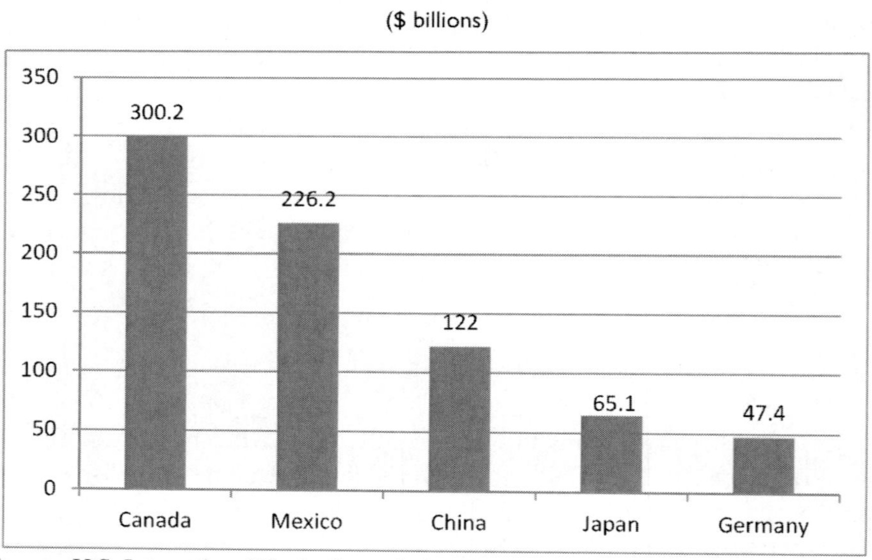

Source: U.S. International Trade Commission DataWeb.

Figure 2. Top 5 U.S. Merchandise Export Markets: 2013.

Table 1. U.S. Merchandise Trade with China: 1980-2013 ($ billions)

Year	U.S. Exports	U.S. Imports	U.S. Trade Balance
1980	3.8	1.1	2.7
1985	3.9	3.9	0.0
1990	4.8	15.2	-10.4
1995	11.7	45.6	-33.8
2000	16.3	100.1	-83.8
2005	41.8	243.5	-201.6
2006	55.2	287.8	-232.5
2007	65.2	321.5	-256.3
2008	71.5	337.8	-266.3
2009	69.6	296.4	-226.8
2010	91.9	364.9	-273.1
2011	103.9	393.3	-295.5
2012	110.6	425.6	-315.0
2013	122.0	440.4	-318.4

Source: U.S. International Trade Commission (USITC) DataWeb.

In addition, China was the second-largest U.S. agricultural export market in 2013 at $27.9 billion. China is also a significant market for U.S. exports of private services. These totaled $30 billion in 2012, making China the fourth-largest export market for U.S. private services.[5]

Many trade analysts argue that China could prove to be a much more significant market for U.S. exports in the future. China is one of the world's fastest-growing economies, and rapid economic growth is likely to continue in the near future, provided that economic reforms are continued.[6] China's goals of modernizing its infrastructure, upgrading its industries, and improving rural living standards could generate substantial demand for foreign goods and services. Finally, economic growth has substantially improved the purchasing power of Chinese citizens, especially those living in urban areas along the east coast of China. China's growing economy, large foreign exchange reserves (at over $3.7 trillion as of September 2013), and large population of over 1.3 billion people make it a potentially enormous market. To illustrate:

Table 2. Major U.S. Exports to China: 2009-2013 ($ millions and percent change)

NAIC Commodity	2009	2010	2011	2012	2013	2012-2013 % change
Total Exports to China	69,576	91,878	103,879	110,590	122,016	10.3%
Oilseeds and grains	9,376	11,208	11,500	16,546	16,092	-2.7%
Aerospace products and parts	5,344	5,766	6,392	8,367	12,620	50.8%
Waste and scrap	7,142	8,561	11,540	9,526	8,765	-8.0%
Motor vehicles	1,134	3,515	5,369	5,788	8,614	48.8%
Navigational, measuring, electro- medical, and controlling instruments	2,917	3,782	4,275	5,153	5,732	11.2%
Semiconductors and other electronic components	6,041	7,555	5,668	4,859	5,724	17.8%
Basic chemicals	3,433	4,202	4,658	4,716	4,934	4.6%
Resin, synthetic rubber, & artificial & synthetic fibers & filament	4,036	4,336	4,476	4,278	4,237	-1.0%
Other general purpose machinery	1,890	2,445	3,113	3,021	3,166	4.8%
Meat products and meat packaging products	1,438	1,319	2,020	2,409	2,759	14.5%

Source: USITC DataWeb.

Note: Top 10 U.S. exports to China in 2013 using the North American Industry Classification (NAIC) System on a 4-digit level.

Table 3. Major U.S. Merchandise Export Markets: 2004-2013 ($ billions and percent change)

Country	2004	2012	2013	Percent Change 2012-2013	Percent Change 2004-2013
Total U.S. Exports	**817**	**1,546**	**1,579**	**2.1%**	**193.3**
Canada	188	292	300	2.9%	159.6%
Mexico	111	216	226	4.5%	203.6%
China	**35**	**111**	**122**	**10.3%**	**348.6%**
Japan	54	70	65	-7.0%	120.4%
Germany	31	49	47	-2.8%	151.6%
UK	36	55	47	-13.6%	130.6%
Brazil	14	44	44	0.9%	314.3%
Netherlands	24	41	43	4.9%	179.2%
Hong Kong	16	37	42	13.3%	262.5%
Korea	26	42	42	-1.8%	161.5%
France	21	31	32	3.7%	152.4%
Belgium	17	29	32	7.9%	188.2%
Singapore	20	31	31	0.5%	155.0%
Switzerland	9	26	27	3.1%	300.0%
Australia	14	31	26	-16.5%	185.7%

Source: U.S. International Trade Commission DataWeb.

Note: Ranked according to the top 10 U.S. export markets in 2013.

- According to a report by the Boston Consulting Group, in 2009, China had 148 million "middle class and affluent" consumers, defined as those whose annual household income was 60,000 RMB ($9,160) or higher, and that level is projected to rise to 415 million by 2020.[7] A May 2013 Boston Consulting Group study estimated that China had 1.3 million millionaires in 2012.[8]
- Although Chinese private consumption as a percent of GDP is much lower than that of most other major economies, the rate of growth of Chinese private consumption has been rising rapidly. For example, private consumption as a percent of GDP in China in 2012 was 36.3%, compared to 71.0% in the United States. However, the annual rate of growth in Chinese private consumption from 2001 to 2012 averaged 8.4%, while the U.S. annual average was 2.0%.[9]

- China's government has indicated that it plans to step up efforts to boost domestic spending to help lessen its dependence on exports as the major contributor to China's economic growth. In 2008, China began the implementation of a $586 billion economic stimulus package, largely focused on infrastructure projects. China's goals of developing its western regions, expanding and modernizing its infrastructure, boosting its social safety net (such as health care and pensions), modernizing and developing key industries, reducing pollution, and raising incomes of the rural poor will likely result in large-scale government spending levels. China's 12th Five-Year Plan (2011-2015) reportedly will allocate $1 trillion to infrastructure spending.[10]
- China currently has the world's largest mobile phone network and one of the fastest-growing markets, with over 1.22 billion mobile phone subscribers as of October 2013.[11]
- Boeing Corporation predicts that over the next 20 years (2013-2032), China will buy 5,580 new commercial airplanes valued at $780 billion and will be Boeing's largest commercial airplane customer outside the United States.[12]
- China replaced the United States as the world's largest Internet user in 2008. At the end of June 2012, China had an estimated 538 million users versus 245 million in the United States. Yet, the percentage of the Chinese population using the Internet is small relative to the United States: 40.1% versus 78.1%, respectively.[13]
- In 2009, China became the world's largest producer of motor vehicles as well as the largest market for new vehicles.
- General Motors (GM) sold more cars and trucks in China than in the United States each year from 2010 to 2013.[14]

Major U.S. Imports from China

China was the largest source of U.S. merchandise imports in 2013, at $440 billion, up 3.5% over the previous year. China's share of total U.S. imports rose from 8.2% in 2000 to 19.1% in 2010, dropped to 18.1% in 2011, but rose to 18.7% in 2012 and to 19.4% in 2013. The importance (ranking) of China as a source of U.S. imports has risen sharply, from eighth largest in 1990, to fourth in 2000, to second in 2004-2006, to first in 2007-2013. The top five U.S. imports from China in 2011 were computer equipment, communications equipment, miscellaneous manufactured products (such as toys and games), apparel, and semiconductors and other electronic parts (see Table 4). China was also the third-largest source of U.S. agricultural imports at $4.6 billion. China was the 10th-largest source of U.S. imports of private services at $13.0 billion in 2012.[15]

Table 4. Major U.S. Merchandise Imports From China: 2009-2013 ($ millions and percent change)

NAIC Commodity	2009	2010	2011	2012	2013	Percent Change 2012 - 2013
Total imports from China	**296,402**	**364,944**	**399,335**	**425,644**	**440,434**	**3.5%**
Computer equipment	44,818	59,800	68,276	68,815	68,123	-0.1%
Communications equipment	26,362	33,464	39,806	51,857	58,839	13.5%
Miscellaneous manufactured commodities	30,668	34,168	32,672	32,644	32,440	-0.6%
Apparel	22,669	26,603	27,554	26,926	27,410	1.8%
Semiconductors and other electronic components	12,363	18,263	19,835	19,012	19,363	1.8%
Footwear	13,119	15,673	16,482	16,870	16,761	-0.6%
Audio and video equipment	18,253	19,493	15,853	15,894	13,830	-13.0%
Household and institutional furniture and kitchen cabinets	9,128	11,123	11,398	12,235	13,225	8.1%
Household appliances and miscellaneous machines	7,724	9,090	9,569	10,298	11,670	13.3%
Motor vehicle parts	4,710	6,966	8,277	9,447	10,441	10.5%

Source: U.S. International Trade Commission DataWeb.

Notes: Top 10 U.S. imports from China in 2013 using the North American Industry Classification (NAIC) System on a 4-digit level.

Throughout the 1980s and 1990s, nearly all U.S. imports from China were low-value, labor-intensive products, such as toys and games, consumer electronic products, footwear, and textiles and apparel. However, over the past few years, an increasing proportion of U.S. imports from China have been comprised of more technologically advanced products (see text box below).

U.S.-China Trade in Advanced Technology Products

According to the U.S. Census Bureau, U.S. imports of "advanced technology products" (ATP) from China in 2013 totaled $145.9 billion. ATP products accounted for 33.1% of total U.S. imports from China, compared with 19.2% ($29.3 billion) in 2003. In addition, ATP imports from China accounted for 36.4% of total U.S ATP imports (compared with 14.1% in 2003). U.S. ATP exports to China in 2013 were $29.1 billion; these accounted for 23.9% of total U.S. exports to China and 9.1% of U.S. global ATP exports. In comparison, U.S. ATP exports to China in 2003 were $8.3 billion, which accounted for 29.2% of U.S. exports to China and 4.6% of total U.S. ATP exports.

The United States ran a $116.8 billion deficit in its ATP trade with China in 2013, up from a $21.0 billion deficit in 2003. Some see the large and growing U.S. trade deficit in ATP with China as a source of concern, contending that it signifies the growing international competitiveness of China in high technology.

Others dispute this, noting that a large share of the ATP imports from China are in fact relatively low-end technology products and parts, such as notebook computers, or are products that are assembled in China using imported high technology parts that are largely developed and/or made elsewhere.

China as a Major Center for Global Supply Chains

Many analysts contend that the sharp increase in U.S. imports from China (and hence the growing bilateral trade imbalance) is largely the result of movement in production facilities from other (primarily Asian) countries to China.

That is, various products that used to be made in such places as Japan, Taiwan, Hong Kong, etc., and then exported to the United States, are now being made in China (in many cases, by foreign firms in China). To illustrate, in 1990, 47.1% of the value of U.S. manufactured imports came from Pacific Rim countries (including China); this figure declined to 46.2% in 2013.[16] Over this period, the share of total U.S. manufactured imports that came from China increased rose from 3.6% to 25.9%. In other words, while China was becoming an increasingly important source for U.S. manufactured imports, the relative importance of the rest of the Pacific Rim (excluding China) as a source of U.S. imports was declining, in part because many multinational firms were shifting their export-oriented manufacturing facilities to China (see Figure 3). In 1990, China accounted for 7.7% of U.S. manufactured imports from all Pacific Rim countries, but by 2013, this figure grew to 55.9%.

Another illustration of the shift in production can be seen in the case of U.S. computer equipment imports, which constitute the largest category of U.S. imports from China (on an NAIC basis, 4-digit level). In 2000, Japan was the largest foreign supplier of U.S. computer equipment (with a 19.6% share of total U.S. imports), while China ranked fourth (with a 12.1% share). By 2013, Japan's ranking had fallen to fourth; the value of its shipments dropped by 70.2% over 2000 levels, and its share of U.S. computer imports declined to 3.8% (2013). China was by far the largest foreign supplier of computer equipment in 2013 with a 64.0% share of total U.S. computer equipment imports, compared to 12.0% in 2000 (see Figure 4). While U.S. imports of computer equipment from China from 2000 to 2013 rose by 725.1%, the total value of U.S. computer imports worldwide rose by only 55.1%.[17] A study by the U.S. International Trade Commission (USITC) estimated that in 2002 over 99% of computer exports in China were from foreign-invested firms in China.[18] Taiwan, one of the world's leaders in sales of information technology, produces over 90% of its information hardware equipment (such as computers) in China. Computer equipment, like many other globally traded products, often involves many stages of production, using parts and other inputs made by numerous multinational firms throughout the world, a significant share of which is assembled in China. The globalization of supply chains makes it increasingly difficult to interpret conventional U.S. trade statistics (see text box below).

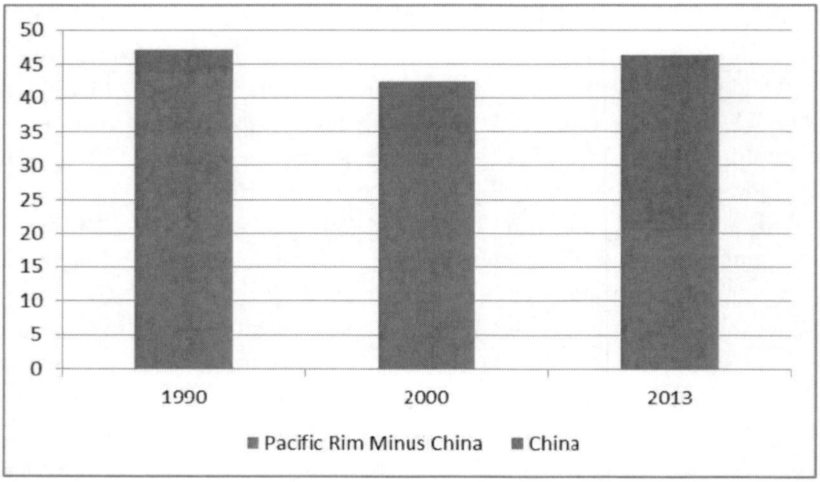

Source: U.S. International Trade Commission DataWeb.

Notes: Standard International Trade Classification (SITC) definition of manufactured imports.

Figure 3. U.S. Manufactured Imports from Pacific Rim Countries as a Percent of Total U.S. Manufactured Imports: 1990, 2000, and 2013.

(percent)

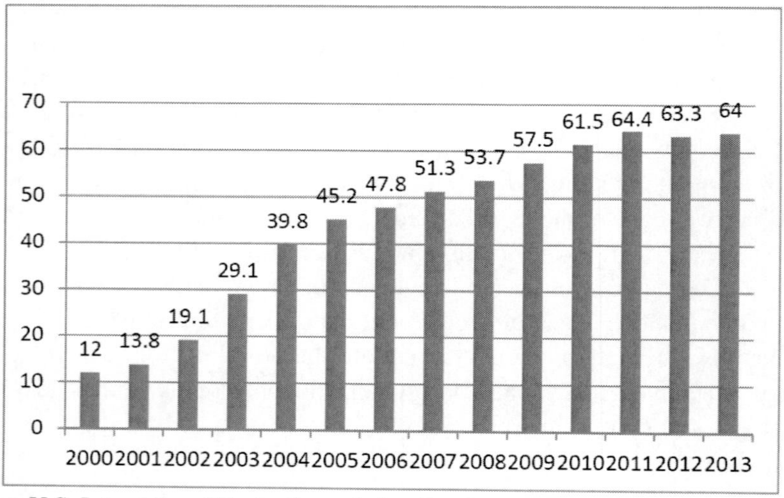

Source: U.S. International Trade Commission DataWeb.

Figure 4. U.S. Computer Imports from China as a Percentage of Total U.S. Computer Imports: 2000-2013.

Global Supply Chains, China, and the Apple iPod: Who Benefits?

Many U.S. companies sign contracts with Taiwanese firms to have their products manufactured (mainly in China), and then shipped to the United States where they are sold by U.S. firms under their own brand name. In many instances, the level of value-added that occurs in China (often it simply involves assemblage) can be quite small relative to the overall cost/price of the final product. One study by researchers at the University of California looked at the production of a 2005 Apple 30 gigabyte video iPod, which is made in China by Foxconn, a Taiwanese company, using parts produced globally (mainly in Asia). The study estimated that it cost about $144 to make each iPod unit. Of this amount, only about $4, or 2.8% of the total cost, was attributable to the Chinese workers who assembled it; the rest of the costs were attributable to the numerous firms involved in making the parts (for example, Japanese firms provided the highest-value components—the hard drive and the display).[19] From a trade aspect, U.S. trade data would have recorded the full value of each iPod unit imported from China at $144 (excluding shipping costs) as originating from China, even though the value added in China was quite small. The retail price of the iPod sold in the United States was $299, meaning that there was a mark-up of about $155 per unit, which was attributable to transportation costs, retail and distributor margins, and Apple's profits. The study estimated that Apple earned at least $80 on each unit it sold in its stores, making it the single largest beneficiary (in terms of gross profit) of the sale of the iPod. The study concluded that Apple's innovation in developing and engineering the iPod and its ability to source most of its production to low-cost countries, such as China, has helped enable it to become a highly competitive and profitable firm (as well as a source for high-paying jobs in the United States). The iPod example illustrates that the rapidly changing nature of global supply chains has made it increasing difficult to interpret the implications of U.S. trade data. Such data may show where products are being imported from, but they often fail to reflect who benefits from that trade. Thus, in many instances, U.S. imports from China are really imports from many countries.

U.S.-China Investment Ties[20]

Investment plays a large and growing role in U.S.-China commercial ties.[21] China's investment in U.S. assets can be broken down into several categories, including holdings of U.S. securities, foreign direct investment (FDI), and other non-bond investments. A significant share of China's investment in the United States is comprised of U.S. securities, while FDI constitutes the bulk of U.S. investment in China. The Treasury Department defines foreign holdings of U.S. securities as "U.S. securities owned by foreign residents (including banks and other institutions) except where the owner has a direct investment relationship with the U.S. issuer of the securities." U.S. statutes define FDI as "the ownership or control, directly or indirectly, by one foreign resident of 10% or more of the voting securities of an incorporated U.S. business enterprise or the equivalent interest in an unincorporated U.S. business enterprise, including a branch."[22] BEA reports data on FDI flows to and from the United States.[23] China has also invested in a number of U.S. companies, projects, and various ventures which do meet the U.S. definition of FDI, and thus, are not reflected in BEA's data.

China's Holdings of U.S. Public and Private Securities[24]

China's holdings of U.S. public and private securities are significant.[25] These include U.S. Treasury securities, U.S. government agency (such as Freddie Mac and Fannie Mae) securities, corporate securities, and equities (such as stocks).China's large holdings of U.S. securities can be largely attributed to its policy of intervening in exchange rate markets to limit the appreciation of its currency to the U.S. dollar (discussed in more detail below). For example, the Chinese government requires Chinese exporters (who are often paid in dollars) to turn over their dollars in exchange for Chinese currency. As a result, the Chinese government has accumulated a significant amount of dollars.[26] Rather than holding onto U.S. dollars, which earn no interest, the Chinese government has chosen to invest many of them into U.S. Treasury securities because they are seen as a relatively safe investment.[27] China's investment in public and private U.S. securities totaled $1.6 trillion as of June 2012.[28]

U.S. Treasury securities, which help the federal government finance its budget deficit, are the largest category of U.S. securities held by China.[29] As indicated in Table 5 and Figure 5, China's holdings of U.S. Treasury securities increased from $118 billion in 2002 to $1.3 trillion as of November 2013, making China the largest foreign holder of U.S. Treasury securities (it overtook Japan as the largest holder in 2008). China's holdings of U.S. Treasury securities as a share of total foreign holdings rose from 9.6% in 2002 to 26.1% in 2010 (year-end), declined to 23.0% in 2011 and to 21.7% in 2012, and then rose to 23.0% as of November 2013.

Some analysts have raised concerns that China's large holdings of U.S. debt securities could give China leverage over U.S. foreign policy, including trade policy. They argue, for example, China might attempt to sell (or threaten to sell) a large share of its U.S. debt securities as punishment over a policy dispute, which could damage the U.S. economy. Others counter that China's holdings of U.S. debt give it very little practical leverage over the United States. They argue that, given China's economic dependency on a stable and growing U.S. economy, and its substantial holdings of U.S. securities, any attempt to try to sell a large share of those holdings would likely damage both the U.S. and Chinese economies. Such a move could also cause the U.S. dollar to sharply depreciate against global currencies, which could reduce the value of China's remaining holdings of U.S. dollar assets. Analysts also note that, while China is the largest foreign owner of U.S. Treasury Securities, those holdings are equal to only 10.4% of total U.S. public debt (as of December 2012). Finally, it is argued that, as long as China continues to largely peg the RMB to the U.S. dollar, it has little choice but to purchase U.S. dollar assets in order to maintain that peg.

Table 5. China's Holdings of U.S. Treasury Securities: 2002-November 2013

	2002	2004	2006	2008	2010	2011	2012	Nov. 2013
China's Holdings ($ billions)	118.0	222.9	396.9	727.4	1,160.1	1,151.9	1,202.8	1,317
China's Holdings as a Percent of Total Foreign Holdings	9.6%	12.1%	18.9%	23.6%	26.1%	23.0%	21.7%	23.0%

Source: U.S. Treasury Department.

Note: Data for 2002-2012 are year-end.

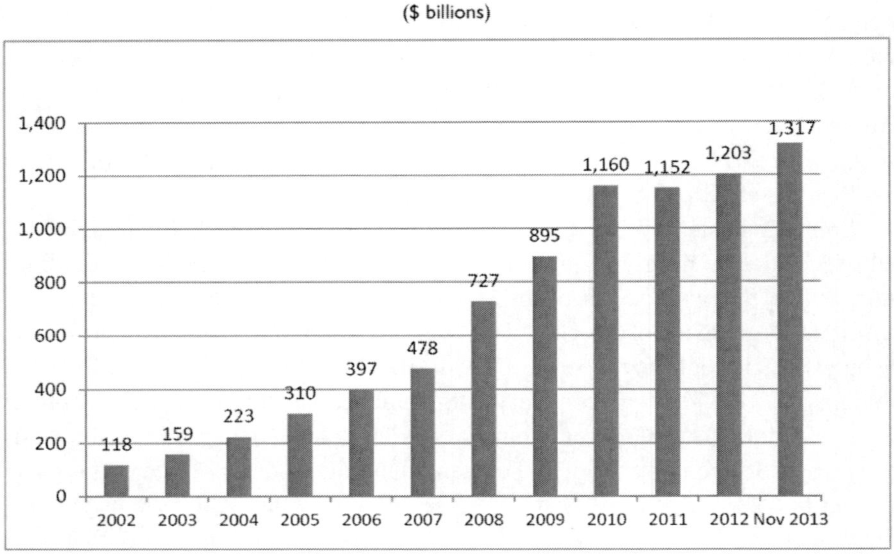

Source: U.S. Department of the Treasury.
Note: Data for 2002-2012 are year-end.

Figure 5. China's Holdings of U.S. Treasury Securities: 2002-November 2013.

In the 112th Congress, the conference report accompanying the National Defense Authorization Act of FY2012 (H.R. 1540, P.L. 112-81) included a provision requiring the Secretary of Defense to conduct a national security risk assessment of U.S. federal debt held by China. The Secretary of Defense issued a report in July 2012, stating that "attempting to use U.S. Treasury securities as a coercive tool would have limited effect and likely would do more harm to China than to the United States." As the threat is not credible and the effect would be limited even if carried out, it does not offer China deterrence options, whether in the diplomatic, military, or economic realms, and this would remain true both in peacetime and in scenarios of crisis or war.[30]

Bilateral Foreign Direct Investment Flows

The level of foreign direct investment (FDI) flows between China and the United States is relatively small given the large volume of trade between the two countries.[31] Many analysts contend that an expansion of bilateral FDI could greatly expand commercial ties.

The U.S. Bureau of Economic Analysis (BEA) is the main federal agency that collects data on FDI flows to and from the United States.[32] Its data indicate that U.S. FDI in China is significantly higher than China's FDI in the United States.[33] BEA reports that the stock of U.S. FDI in China through 2012 was $51.4 billion, down from $59.0 billion in 2010, reflecting an outflow of funds (divestment) from China back to the United States.[34] BEA estimates that U.S. majority-owned affiliates in China employed 1.4 million workers in China in 2011, of which 690,000 were in manufacturing.[35]

BEA's main FDI data measurement puts the stock of Chinese FDI in the United States through the end of 2012 at $5.2 billion on a historical-cost (or book value) basis. In 2012, Chinese FDI flows to the United States were $1.4 billion. However, these data do not reflect FDI that Chinese investors may have made through offshore locations (such as Hong Kong) to invest in the United States. To reflect this, the BEA attempts to measure the level of FDI inflows according to the country of "ultimate beneficial owner" (UBO). These measurements nearly double the estimated level of Chinese FDI in the United States. On a UBO basis, cumulative Chinese FDI in the United States through 2012 was $10.5 billion (see **Table 6**). As indicated in **Figure 6**, the stock of Chinese FDI in the United States on a UBO basis has risen sharply since 2009.

Table 6. U.S. Data on Annual U.S.–China Bilateral FDI Flows: 2005-2012 and Cumulative Value of FDI at Year-End 2012 ($ millions)

	2005	**2006**	**2007**	**2008**	**2009**	**2010**	**2011**	**2012**	**Cumulative: Value of FDI at 2012 Year-End**
China's FDI in the United States	146	315	8	500	500	1,037	520	1,370	5,154 ($10,465)*
U.S. FDI in China	1,955	4,226	5,243	15,971	-7,512	5,240	-1,087	-3,482	51,363

Source: U.S. Bureau of Economic Analysis.

Notes: Cumulative data are on a historical-cost basis.

* Data in parenthesis are BEA estimates of Chinese FDI in the United States that is made by Chinese investors both directly or through other countries, described as the "country of ultimate beneficial owner" (UBO).

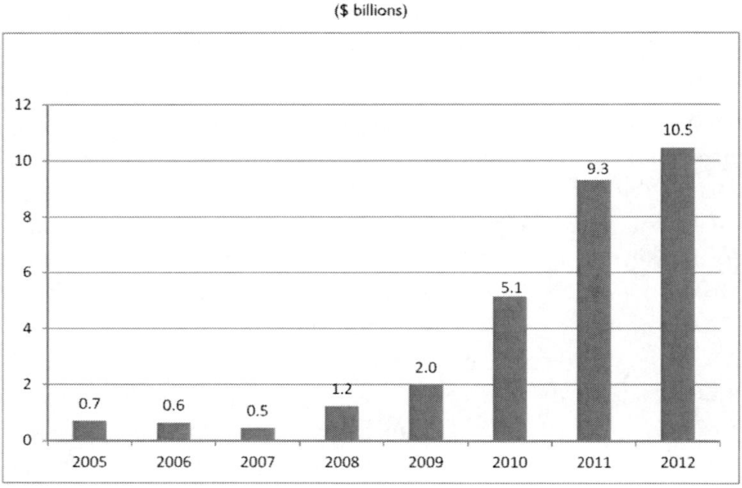

Source: U.S. Bureau of Economic Analysis.

Notes: Data is on a historic-cost basis. UBO data represents estimates of the country of origin of the entity that ultimately owns or controls the U.S. affiliate.

Figure 6. BEA's Estimate of Cumulative Chinese FDI in the United States on a UBO Basis: 2005-2012.

Some analysts contend that the BEA's data on China's FDI in the United States do not fully capture all investments. For example, the Rhodium Group (a private research consultancy and advisory company) estimates that annual Chinese FDI in the United States rose from $1.9 billion in 2009 to $7.1 billion in 2012, to $14 billion in 2013. They estimate the stock of Chinese FDI in the United States from 2000 to 2012 at $23.6 billion (and through 2013at $35.9 billion).[36] As indicated in Figure 7, Rhodium Group's estimates of the stock of Chinese FDI in the United States are significantly higher than BEA's data.

Chinese Companies in the United States

Although the level of Chinese FDI in the United States is relatively small, many Chinese firms view the United States as a key part of their efforts to become more globally competitive companies, move closer to their U.S. customers, circumvent perceived trade and investment barriers (such as the Buy American Act), and avoid U.S. trade remedy measures (such as antidumping duties). Some examples of Chinese FDI in the United States include the following:

The Dalian Wanda Group Corporation Ltd. on May 21, 2011, announced that it had signed a merger and acquisition agreement to acquire AMC Entertainment (the world's second-largest theater chain) for $2.6 billion.

Suntech Power Holdings Co., Ltd., the world's largest producer of solar panels, opened a solar plant in Goodyear, Arizona, in October 2010, employing 100 workers. However, in March 2013, the company announced it planned to close the plant, citing higher production costs exacerbated by U.S. anti-dumping import duties imposed on solar cells and aluminum, as well as global solar module oversupply.[37]

Sany Group, a global producer of construction equipment, founded Sany America Inc. in 2006, headquartered in Peachtree City, Georgia. In 2007, it announced it would invest $100 million to create and establish a manufacturing facility for constructing and engineering Sany products, with expected employment of 300 workers by the time the project is completed.[38]

Wanxiang Group, an automotive parts manufacturer, established Wanxiang America Corporation in 1994, based in Illinois. Over the past decade, Wanxiang America reportedly has purchased or invested in more than 20 U.S. firms and employs 5,000 U.S. workers—more than any other Chinese company.[39] In January 2013, Wanxiang America acquired nearly all of A123 Systems, a manufacturer of advanced lithium-ion batteries, for $256.6 million.

Pacific Centuries Motor (now a subsidiary of AVIC Automobile Industry Co., Ltd, a state-owned firm) purchased Nexteer Automotive, a Michigan-based firm that producers steering and driveline systems, for an estimated $450 million.[40]

Tianjin Pipe Corporation, China's largest steel pipe-maker, announced in 2009 that it planned to spend $1 billion to construct a mini-mill facility in Gregory, Texas, that will manufacture steel products from recycled scrap steel. Over the first 10 years of operation, the project is projected to boost the local economy by $2.7 billion and generate $327 million in direct employee salaries.[41]

Haier Group, a major global appliance and electronics firm, maintains its corporate headquarters for Haier America in New York City, has sales offices in 13 U.S. states, and operates a $40 million refrigerator plant in Camden, South Carolina (employing 120 people), reportedly the first U.S. manufacturing facility built by a Chinese firm (2000).

ZTE Corporation, one of China's largest telecommunications manufacturers, established a U.S. presence in 1995. ZTE USA is headquartered in Dallas, Texas, and maintains R&D facilities in five U.S. states.

Huawei Technologies is a leading global information and communications technology solutions provider. Since gaining a U.S. presence in 2011, Huawei has reportedly partnered with 280 U.S. technology providers, with total procurement contracts exceeding $30 billion, covering such items as software, components, chipsets, and services. In February 2012, Huawei announced procurement contracts with U.S. firms worth $6 billion.[42]

Golden Dragon Precise Copper Tube Group Inc., one of the world's largest precise copper tube manufacturers, announced in February 2012 that it planned to build a $100 million manufacturing facility in Alabama.

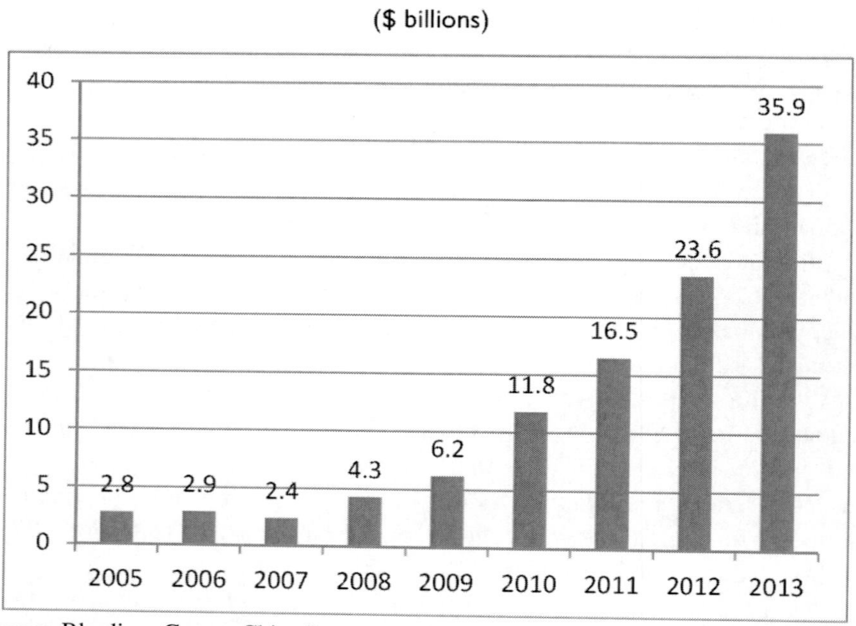

Source: Rhodium Group, China Investment Monitor.

Notes: Data are on a UBO basis and are derived from a number of sources, including commercial databases, media reports, and industry contacts in China.

Figure 7. Rhodium Group's Estimates of Cumulative Chinese FDI in the United States on a UBO Basis: 2005-2013.

In addition to China's FDI in the United States and its holdings in U.S. Treasury securities, China (as of June 2012) held $221 billion in U.S. equities (such as stocks), up from $3 billion in June 2005. It also held $202 billion in U.S. agency securities, many of which are asset-backed (such as Fannie Mae and Freddie Mac securities),[43] and $22 billion in corporate bonds. The China Investment Corporation (CIC), a sovereign wealth fund established by the Chinese government in 2007 with $200 billion in registered capital to help better manage China's foreign exchange reserves, had financial assets totaling $482 billion at the end of 2011. CIC has been one of the largest Chinese purchasers of U.S. equities and other U.S. assets; it has stakes in such firms as Morgan Stanley, the Blackstone Group, and J.C. Flowers & Co.[44] It appears that many of the investments by the CIC and other Chinese entities have attempted to avoid political controversy in the United States by limiting their ownership shares to less than 10%.

Issues Raised by Chinese FDI in the United States

Many U.S. analysts contend that greater Chinese FDI in the United States, especially in "greenfield" projects (new ventures) that manufacture products or provide services in the United States and create new jobs for U.S. workers,[45] could help improve bilateral economic relations and might lessen perceptions among some critics in the United States that growing U.S.-China trade undermines U.S. employment and harms U.S. economic interests.[46] A number of analysts note that China's outward FDI has been growing rapidly since 2004 and is likely to continue in the years ahead.[47]

Such analysts contend that greater efforts should be made by U.S. policy makers to encourage Chinese firms to invest in the United States rather than block them for political reasons. In June 2011, President Obama issued an executive order establishing the "Select USA Initiative" to coordinate federal efforts to promote and retain investment in the United States. According to a White House factsheet issued during the U.S. visit of Chinese Vice President Xi Jinping in February 2012, China was already one of Select USA top 10 focus markets, and the Administration was planning a significant expansion of the initiative, including with resources dedicated to attracting Chinese investors and facilitating their investment. The two sides further pledged to deepen cooperation on infrastructure financing.[48] At the July 2013 session of the U.S.-China S&ED, the United States pledged to welcome investment from China, including those made by Chinese state-owned enterprises (SOEs).

Some critics of China's current FDI policies and practices contend that they are largely focused on mergers and acquisitions that are geared toward boosting the competitive position of Chinese firms and enterprises favored by the Chinese government for development (some of which also may be receiving government subsidies). Some argue that such investments are often made largely to obtain technology and know-how for Chinese firms, but do little to boost the U.S. economy by, for example, building new factories and hiring workers. Another major issue relating to Chinese FDI in the United States is the relative lack of transparency of Chinese firms, especially in terms of their connections to the central government. When Chinese SOEs attempt to purchase U.S. company assets, some U.S. analysts ask what role government officials in Beijing played in that decision. Chinese officials contend that investment decisions by Chinese companies, including SOEs and publicly held firms (where the government is the largest shareholder), are solely based on commercial considerations, and have criticized U.S. investment policies as "protectionist."

According to the Foreign Investment and National Security Act (FINSA) of 2007 (P.L. 110-149), the Committee on Foreign Investment in the United States (CFIUS) may conduct an investigation on the effect of an investment transaction on national security if the covered transaction is a foreign government-controlled transaction (in addition to if the transaction threatens to impair national security, or results in the control of a critical piece of U.S. infrastructure by a foreign person).[49] The House report on the bill (H.Rept. 110-24, H.R. 556) noted: "The Committee believes that acquisitions by certain government-owned companies do create heightened national security concerns, particularly where government-owned companies make decisions for inherently governmental—as opposed to commercial—reasons."

There have been several instances in which efforts by Chinese firms (oftentimes these have been SOEs or state-favored firms) have raised concerns of some U.S. policy makers and/or U.S. stakeholders:

- On January 23, 2014, Lenovo, a Chinese technology company, announced that it would purchase IBM's x86 server business for $2.3 billion. On January 29, 2014, Lenovo announced that it would acquire Motorola Mobility from Google for $2.9 billion.
- On May 29, 2013, Shuanghui International Holdings, the majority owner of China's largest meat processing enterprise (Henan Shuanghui Investment & Development Company), announced it was seeking to purchase Smithfield Foods, the largest U.S. pork producer,

for $7.1 billion (including the assumption of Smithfield's debt). If the merger goes through, it would represent the largest acquisition of a U.S. firm by a Chinese company to date. The proposed acquisition has raised a number of concerns among some U.S. policy makers.[50] On June 20, 2013, 15 members of the Senate Committee on Agricultural, Nutrition, and Forestry sent a letter to the U.S. Secretary of the Treasury contending that the U.S. food supply is "critical infrastructure" and should be regarded as a national security issue during the CFIUS review process, urging that the Department of Agriculture and the Food and Drug Administration be represented in any CFIUS review of the transaction, and stating that review look to broader issues, including food security, food safety, and biosecurity.[51] The Senate Agriculture Committee also announced plans to hold a hearing on the transaction and to "more broadly examine how the government review process of foreign acquisitions of U.S. companies addresses American food safety, protection of American technologies, and intellectual property, and the effects of increased foreign ownership of the U.S. food supply."[52] In a June 21, 2013, letter to Administration officials, Senators Max Baucus and Orrin Hatch stated that the planned acquisition "has thrown a spotlight on China's unjustified trade barriers to U.S. meat exports."[53] A letter sent to Administration officials by Representative Rosa DeLauro and Senator Elizabeth Warren about the planned acquisition on June 26, 2013, raised a number of issues relating to food security, food safety, intellectual property rights protection, unfair Chinese trade practices, and U.S. global economic competitiveness and requested the Obama Administration to publicly respond to eight major concerns.[54] On July 10, 2013, the Senate Committee on Agricultural, Nutrition, and Forestry held a hearing on the proposed transaction. On September 26, 2013, Shuanghui International Holdings completed its purchase of Smithfield.

- In January 2013, Wanxiang America Corporation completed its acquisition of substantially all nongovernment business assets of A123 Systems, a manufacturer of lithium battery products. The acquisition includedA123's automotive, grid, and commercial business assets, including technology, products, customer contracts, and U.S. facilities in Michigan, Massachusetts, and Missouri; its manufacturing operations in China; and its equity interest in Shanghai Advanced Traction Battery Systems Company (A123's joint venture with Shanghai Automotive).[55] Several Members of Congress expressed concerns over the national security implications of Wanxiang's acquisition of A123 Systems, as well as concerns that U.S. government grants that had been given to A123 Systems in the past might end up benefiting a Chinese company.

- On October 8, 2012, the chairman and ranking Member of the House Intelligence Committee (Representatives Mike Rogers and C.A. Dutch Ruppersberger) released a report recommending that U.S. companies considering doing business with Chinese telecommunications companies Huawei and ZTE to find another vendor, and that the CFIUS should block acquisitions, takeovers, or mergers involving Huawei and ZTE given "the threat to U.S. national security interests." The report went on to state that "we have serious concerns about Huawei and ZTE, and their connection to the communist government of China. China is known to be the major perpetrator of cyber espionage, and Huawei and ZTE failed to alleviate serious concerns throughout this important investigation."[56]
- On September 28, 2012, President Obama issued an executive order requiring Ralls Corporation, a Chinese-owned firm, to divest its interest in four wind farm project companies in Oregon that it acquired earlier in the year, due to national security concerns, reportedly because of their proximity to a naval test facility.[57] China's government-controlled media called the action "protectionist."
- On May 9, 2012, the Federal Reserve announced that it had approved (1) the application by Industrial and Commercial Bank of China Limited, China Investment Corporation, and Central Huijin Investment Ltd., to become bank holding companies by acquiring up to 80% of the voting shares of the Bank of East Asia (USA) National Association; (2) the Bank of China's application to establish a branch in Chicago, IL; and (3) the application by the Agricultural Bank of China Limited to establish a state-licensed branch in New York City.[58] In a letter to Federal Reserve Chairman Ben Bernanke, Senator Robert Casey noted that each of the entities approved by the Federal Reserve was state-owned, and he expressed concern that "these banks and their U.S. subsidiaries will use their state-support as a way to underprice U.S. banks that abide by U.S. law and do not have the support of a sovereign country behind them."[59]
- In May 2010, Huawei bought certain intellectual property assets of 3Leaf Systems (an insolvent U.S. technology firm) for $2 million.

A February 2011 letter issued by Senators Jim Webb and Jon Kyl to then-Commerce Secretary Gary Locke and then-Treasury Secretary Tim Geithner stated: "We are convinced that any attempt Huawei makes to expand its presence in the U.S. or acquire U.S. companies warrants thorough scrutiny. Moreover, the 3Leaf acquisition appears certain to generate transfer to China by Huawei of advanced U.S. computing technology. Allowing Huawei and, by extension, communist China to have access to this core technology could pose a serious risk as U.S. computer networks come to further rely on and integrate this technology."[60] In February 2011, Huawei stated that it been formally notified by CFIUS that it should withdraw its application to acquire 3Leaf's assets, which it later did.[61] In an "Open Letter," Huawei invited the U.S. government to carry out a formal investigation on any concerns it may have about Huawei.[62]

- In May 2010, Anshan Iron and Steel Group Corporation (Ansteel), a major Chinese state-owned steel producer, announced plans to form a joint venture with Steel Development Company, a U.S. firm in Mississippi, to build and operate four mills to produce reinforcing bar and other bar products used in infrastructure applications, and one mill that would be capable of producing electrical and silicon grades of steel used in energy applications.[63] In July 2010, the Congressional Steel Caucus sent a letter signed by 50 Members to Secretary of the Treasury Tim Geithner, expressing concerns over the effect the investment would have "on American jobs and our national security."[64] At a February 2012 hearing on China's SOEs, Representative Visclosky, chairman of the Congressional Steel Caucus stated: "As a Caucus, we were concerned that the investment would allow a Chinese state-owned enterprise to pursue the government of China's aims, and not the aims of the employer, the American worker, or the market. We were concerned that this investment would allow the full force and financing of the Chinese government to exploit the American steel market from American soil. We also were concerned that China would have access to new steel production technologies and information regarding American national security infrastructure projects."[65]
- In February 2010, Emcore Corporation, a provider of compound semiconductor-based components, subsystems, and systems for the fiber optics and solar power markets, announced it had agreed to sell 60% interest in its fiber optics business (excluding its satellite

communications and specialty photonics fiber optics businesses) to China's Tangshan Caofeidian Investment Corporation (TCIC) for $27.8 million. However, Emcore announced in June 2010 that the deal had been ended because of concerns by CFIUS.[66]

- In July 2009, China's Northwest Nonferrous International Investment Company, a Chinese SOE, made a $26 million offer to purchase a 51% stake in the Firstgold Corporation, a U.S. exploration-stage company. However, the deal reportedly raised national concerns within CFUIS because some of the mines controlled by Firstgold were near U.S. military installations. As a result, the Chinese firm withdrew its bid in December 2009.[67]
- In September 2007, Huawei announced plans, along with its partner, Bain Capital Partners, to buy the U.S. firm 3Com Corporation, a provider of data networking equipment, for $2.2 billion. However, the proposed merger was withdrawn in February 2008 following a review of the deal by CFIUS when Huawei and its partner failed to adequately address U.S. national security concerns raised by CFIUS members.[68]

In 2005, the China National Offshore Oil Corporation (CNOOC), a Chinese SOE, made a bid to buy UNOCAL, a U.S. energy company, for $18.5 billion, but widespread opposition in Congress led CNOOC to withdraw its bid. Some Members argued at the time that the proposed takeover represented a clear threat to the energy and national security of the United States, would put vital oil assets in the Gulf of Mexico and Alaska into the hands of a Chinese state-controlled company, could transfer a host of highly advanced technologies to China, and that CNOOC's bid to take over UNOCAL would be heavily subsidized by the Chinese government. Some Members argued that "vital" U.S. energy assets should never sold to the Chinese government. CNOOC officials referred to U.S. political opposition to the sale as "regrettable and unjustified."[69]

- In 2004, Lenovo Group Limited, a computer company primarily owned by the Chinese government, signed an agreement with IBM Corporation to purchase IBM's personal computer division for $1.75 billion. Some U.S. officials raised national security concerns over potential espionage activities that could occur in the United States at IBM research facilities by Lenovo employees if the deal went through. A review of the agreement by CFIUS took place in which IBM and Lenovo were able to address certain national security concerns and, as a result, the acquisition was completed in April 2005.[70]

Chinese Restrictions on U.S. FDI in China

U.S. trade officials have urged China to liberalize its FDI regime in order to boost U.S. business opportunities in, and expand U.S. exports to, China. Although China is one of the world's top recipients of FDI, the Chinese central government imposes numerous restrictions on the level and of types of FDI allowed in China. According to the U.S.-China Business Council, China imposes ownership barriers on nearly 100 industries.[71] The OECD's 2012 FDI Regulatory Restrictiveness Index, which measures statutory restrictions on foreign direct investment in 57 countries (including all OECD and G20 countries, and covering 22 sectors), ranked China's FDI regime as the most restrictive, based on foreign equity limitations, screening or approval mechanisms, restrictions on the employment of foreigners as key personnel, and operational restrictions (such as restrictions on branching, capital repatriation, and land ownership).[72]

To a great extent, China's investment policies appear to be linked to industrial policies that seek to promote the development of sectors identified by the government as critical to future economic development. For example, since the early 1980s, the Chinese government has encouraged foreign auto companies to invest in China, but has limited FDI in that sector to 50-50 joint ventures with domestic Chinese partners.[73] In addition, the central government maintains a "Guideline Catalogue for Foreign Investment" (the latest revision was issued in January 2012), which lists FDI categories that are encouraged, restricted, or prohibited.[74] Many of the sectors under the "encouraged" category include high technology, green technology, and energy conservation, and pollution control.[75] Several of the sectors under the "restricted" category limit FDI to joint ventures (such as for rare earth smelting) or where the Chinese parties are the controlling shareholders (such as railway passenger transport companies). "Prohibited" sectors are those that fall under "national security" concerns (such as manufacturing of ammunition and weapons) or are categories where the government seeks to preserve state monopolies (such as postal companies) or protect Chinese firms from foreign competition (such as mining of rare earth elements).

The Chinese government also sets restrictions on FDI inflows during the investment screening process, or through its mergers and acquisition regulations, especially when seeking to protect pillar or strategic industries that the central government (as well as many provincial and local governments) seeks to promote. Many critics of China's investment policies contend that the Chinese government often requires foreign firms to transfer technology to their China partners, and sometimes to set up research and development facilities in China, in exchange for access to China's markets.[76] Foreign-invested firms in China face a number of challenges, including local protectionism, lack of regulatory transparency, IPR theft, and discriminatory license practices. A 2013 business survey by the American Chamber of Commerce in China (AmCham China) found that 35% of respondents stated that they were at a competitive disadvantage as a result of Chinese industrial policies that favored state-owned enterprises.[77] Some U.S. policy makers have suggested that Chinese investment in certain U.S. sectors should be restricted in response to Chinese policies that limit U.S. FDI in China in similar sectors.[78]

The United States and China have held negotiations on reaching a bilateral investment treaty (BIT) with the goal of expanding bilateral investment opportunities. U.S. negotiators hope such a treaty would improve the investment climate for U.S. firms in China by enhancing legal protections and dispute resolution procedures, and by obtaining a commitment from the Chinese government that it would treat U.S. investors no less favorably than Chinese investors. However, some groups have argued that a BIT with China could hurt U.S. workers by encouraging more U.S. firms to relocate to China.[79]

In April 2012, the Obama Administration released a "Model Bilateral Investment Treaty" that was developed to enhance U.S. objectives in the negotiation of new BITs.[80] The new BIT model establishes mechanisms to promote greater transparency, labor and environment requirements, disciplines to prevent parties from imposing domestic technology requirements, and measures to boost the ability of investors to participate in the development of standards and technical regulations on a nondiscriminatory basis.

During the July 10-11, 2013, session of the U.S.-China Strategic and Economic Dialogue (S&ED), China indicated its intention to negotiate a high-standard BIT with the United States that would include all stages of investment and all sectors, a move that U.S. officials described as "a significant breakthrough, and the first time China has agreed to do so with another country."[81] A press release by the Chinese Ministry of Commerce stated that China was willing to negotiate a BIT on the basis of non-discrimination and a negative list, meaning the agreement would identify only those sectors not open to foreign investment on a non-discriminatory basis (as opposed to a BIT with a positive list which would only list sectors open to foreign investment).

At the Communist Party of China's 3rd Plenum meeting in November 2013, the government stated that it would reduce regulations on FDI in China and create a number of free trade zones that may open up certain sectors to foreign investment.

MAJOR U.S.-CHINA TRADE ISSUES

China's economic reforms and rapid economic growth, along with the effects of globalization, have caused the economies of the United States and China to become increasingly integrated.[82] Although growing U.S.-China economic ties are considered by most analysts to be mutually beneficial overall, tensions have risen over a number of Chinese economic and trade policies that many U.S. critics charge are protectionist, economically distortive, and damaging to U.S. economic interests. According to the USTR, most U.S. trade disputes with China stem from the consequences of its incomplete transition to a free market economy. Major areas of concern for U.S. stakeholders include China's:

- Extensive network of industrial policies that seek to promote and protect domestic sectors and firms, especially SOEs, deemed by the government to be critical to the country's future economic growth;
- Failure to provide adequate protection of U.S. intellectual property rights (IPR) and (alleged) government-directed cyber security attacks against U.S. firms;
- Mixed record on implementing its obligations in the World Trade Organization (WTO) and its failure to date to join the WTO's Government Procurement Agreement (GPA); and
- Intervention in currency markets to limit the appreciation of the renminbi (RMB) against the dollar (and other major currencies) in order to make China's exports more globally competitive.

Chinese "State Capitalism"

Currently, a significant share of China's economy is thought to be driven by market forces. According to a 2010 WTO report, the private sector now accounts for more than 60% of China's gross domestic product (GDP).[83] However, the Chinese government continues to play a major role in economic decision-making. For example, at the macroeconomic level, the Chinese government maintains policies that induce households to save a high level of their income, much of which is deposited in state-controlled Chinese banks. This enables the government to provide low-cost financing to Chinese firms, especially SOEs. At the microeconomic level, the Chinese government (at the central and local government level) seeks to promote the development of industries that are deemed critical to the country's future economic development by using various policies, such as subsidies, tax breaks, preferential loans, trade barriers, FDI restrictions, discriminatory regulations and standards, export restrictions on raw materials (such as rare earths), technology transfer requirements imposed on foreign firms, public procurement rules that give preferences to domestic firms, and weak enforcement of IPR laws.

Many analysts contend that the Chinese government's intervention in various sectors through industrial policies has intensified in recent years. The December 2013 U.S. Trade Representative's (USTR's) report on China's WTO trade compliance states:

> During most of the past decade, the Chinese government emphasized the state's role in the economy, diverging from the path of economic reform that had driven China's accession to the WTO. With the state leading China's economic development, the Chinese government pursued new and more expansive industrial policies, often designed to limit market access for imported goods, foreign manufacturers and foreign service suppliers, while offering substantial government guidance, resources and regulatory support to Chinese industries, particularly ones dominated by state-owned enterprises. This heavy state role in the economy, reinforced by unchecked discretionary actions of Chinese government regulators, generated serious trade frictions with China's many trade partners, including the United States.[84]

The extent of SOE involvement in the Chinese economy is difficult to measure due to the opaque nature of the corporate sector in China and the relative lack of transparency regarding the relationship between state actors (including those at the central and non-central government levels) and Chinese firms. According to one study by the U.S.-China Economic and Security Review Commission:

> The state sector in China consists of three main components. First, there are enterprises fully owned by the state through the State-owned Assets and Supervision and Administration Commission (SASAC) of the State Council and by SASACs of provincial, municipal, and county governments. Second, there are SOEs that are majority owners of enterprises that are not officially considered SOEs but are effectively controlled by their SOE owners. Finally, there is a group of entities, owned and controlled indirectly through SOE subsidiaries based inside and outside of China. The actual size of this third group is unknown. Urban collective enterprises and government-owned township and village enterprises (TVEs) also belong to the state sector but are not considered SOEs. The state-owned and controlled portion of the Chinese economy is large. Based on reasonable assumptions, it appears that the visible state sector—SOEs and entities directly controlled by SOEs, accounted for more than 40 percent of China's nonagricultural GDP. If the contributions of indirectly controlled entities, urban collectives, and public TVEs are considered, the share of GDP owned and controlled by the state is approximately 50 percent.[85]

According to the Chinese government, at the end of 2011, there were 144,700 state-owned or state-controlled enterprises, excluding financial institutions, with total assets worth $13.6 trillion.[86] Chinese SOEs have undergone significant restructuring over the years. More than 90% of SOEs have reportedly become corporations or shareholding companies.[87] The Chinese government has identified a number of industries where the state should have full control or where the state should dominate. These include autos, aviation, banking, coal, construction, environmental technology, information technology, insurance, media, metals (such as steel), oil and gas, power, railways, shipping, telecommunications, and tobacco.[88]

Many SOEs are owned or controlled by local governments. According to one analyst:

> The typical large industrial Chinese company is...wholly or majority-owned by a local government which appoints senior management and provides free or low-cost land and utilities, tax breaks, and where possible, guarantees that locally made products will be favored by local governments, consumers, and other businesses. In return, the enterprise

provides the local state with a source of jobs for local workers, tax revenues, and dividends.[89]

China's banking system is largely controlled by state-owned or state-controlled banks. In 2011, the top five largest banks in China, all of which were shareholding companies with significant state ownership, accounted for 57.5% of Chinese banking assets. The Chinese government also has four banks that are 100% state-owned and holds shares in a number of joint stock commercial banks.[90] SOEs are believed to receive preferential credit treatment by government banks, while private firms must often pay higher interest rates or obtain credit elsewhere. According to one estimate, SOEs accounted for 85% ($1.4 trillion) of all bank loans in 2009.[91]

Not only are SOEs dominant players in China's economy, many are becoming quite large by global standards. In 2013, 84 Chinese companies (excluding Hong Kong firms) made *Fortune Magazine's Global 500* list of the world's largest firms based on revenues. Of the 84 Chinese companies listed, 77 firms or 88.1% were state-owned or state-controlled enterprises (defined as where the state owned 50% of the company). Of the 10 non-SOEs companies listed, at least 3 are partially owned by the government. For example, the government owes 26.5% of the Bank of Communications, 15.7% of China Minsheng Banking Corp., and 20% of Shanghai Pudong Development Bank.[92] Another company, Huawei (a major telecommunications company) describes itself as an employee-owned firm. However, many U.S. analysts contend that Huawei has strong links with the Chinese government, including the Chinese People's Liberation Army (PLA), and has not published a full breakdown of its ownership structure. In addition, in the past, the Chinese government reportedly ordered state banks to extend loans to the company early in its development so that it could compete against foreign firms in the domestic telecommunications market.[93]

China's Plan to Modernize the Economy and Promote Indigenous Innovation

Many of the industrial policies that China has implemented or formulated since 2006 appear to stem largely from a comprehensive document issued by China's State Council (the highest executive organ of state power) in 2006 titled the *National Medium-and Long-Term Program for Science and Technology Development (2006-2020)*, often referred to as the MLP. The MLP appears to represent an ambitious plan to modernize the structure of China's economy by transforming it from a global center of low-tech manufacturing to a major center of innovation (by the year 2020) and a global innovation leader by 2050.[94] It also seeks to sharply reduce the country's dependence on foreign technology. The MLP includes the stated goals of "indigenous innovation, leapfrogging in priority fields, enabling development, and leading the future."[95] Some of the broad goals of the MLP state that by 2020:

- The progress of science and technology will contribute 60% or above to China's development.
- The country's reliance on foreign technology will decline to 30% or below (from an estimated current level of 50%).
- Gross expenditures for research and development (R&D) would rise to 2.5% of gross domestic product (from 1.3% in 2005). Priority areas for increased R&D include space programs, aerospace development and manufacturing, renewable energy, computer science, and life sciences.[96]

The document states that "China must place the strengthening of indigenous innovative capability at the core of economic restructuring, growth model change, and national competitiveness enhancement. Building an innovation-oriented country is therefore a major strategic choice for China's future development." This goal, according to the document, is to be achieved by formulating and implementing regulations in the country's government procurement law to "encourage and protect indigenous innovation," establishing a coordination mechanism for government procurement of indigenous innovative products, requiring a first-buy policy for major domestically made high-tech equipment and products that possess proprietary intellectual property rights, providing policy support to enterprises in procuring domestic high-tech equipment, and developing "relevant technology standards" through government procurement.

Reaction by U.S. Stakeholders

Beginning in 2009, several U.S. companies began to raise concerns over a number of Chinese government circulars that would establish an "Indigenous Innovation Product Accreditation" system. For example, in November 2009, the Chinese government released a "Circular on Launching the 2009 National Indigenous Innovation Product Accreditation Work," requiring companies to file applications by December 2009 for their products to be considered for accreditation as "indigenous innovation products." Similar proposed circulars were issued at the provincial and local government levels as well. U.S.

business representatives expressed deep concern over the circulars, arguing that they were protectionist in nature because they extended preferential treatment for Chinese government procurement to domestic Chinese firms that developed and owned intellectual property (IP) and thus largely excluded foreign firms.[97] AmCham China described China's attempt to link IP ownership with market access as "unprecedented worldwide."[98] A letter written by the U.S. Chamber of Commerce and 33 business associations to the Chinese government on December 10, 2009, stated that the indigenous innovations circulars would "make it virtually impossible for any non-Chinese companies to participate in China's government procurement market—even those that have made substantial and long-term investments in China, employ Chinese citizens, and pay taxes to the Chinese government."[99] Such groups contend that a large share of their technology is developed globally and thus it would be difficult to attribute the share of technology developed in China needed to obtain accreditation.[100]

A 2011 AmCham China survey found that 40% of respondents believed that China's indigenous innovation policies would hurt their businesses and 26% said their businesses were already being hurt by such policies. At a November 2011 WTO review of China's IPR policies, the U.S. WTO representative stated that China's policies of adopting indigenous innovation had "created a troubling trend toward increased discriminatory policies which were aimed at coercing technology transfer." He stated that "Chinese regulations, rules and other regulatory measures frequently called for technology transfer, and in certain cases, conditioned, or proposed to condition, the eligibility for government benefits or preferences on intellectual property being owned or developed in China, or being licensed, in some cases exclusively, to a Chinese party."[101]

China's Response to U.S. Concerns

The Chinese government responded to U.S. concerns over its indigenous innovation policies by arguing that they did not discriminate against foreign firms or violate global trade rules.[102] However, during the visit of (then) Chinese President Hu Jintao to the United States in January 2011, the Chinese government stated that it would not link its innovation policies to the provision of government procurement preferences.[103] During the May 2011 session of the U.S.-China Strategic and Economic Dialogue (S&ED), China pledged that it would eliminate all of its indigenous innovation products catalogs.[104] During the November 2011 talks held under the U.S.-China Joint Commission on Commerce and Trade (JCCT), the Chinese government announced that the

State Council had issued a measure requiring governments of provinces, municipalities, and autonomous regions to eliminate by December 1, 2011, any catalogues or other measures linking innovation policies to government procurement preferences.[105] This occurred after foreign business groups raised concerns that discriminatory indigenous innovation policies might continue to be implemented at the local level even after Hu Jintao's commitment. For example, The U.S.-China Business Council (USCBC) reported in February 2011 that it had identified 22 municipal and provincial governments that had issued at least 61 indigenous innovation catalogues. U.S. business representatives sought to ensure that Beijing's pledge on indigenous innovation would apply at all levels of government in China.

In May 2013, the USCBC reported that, although the central government had largely been successful in ensuring that sub-national governments complied with implement Hu Jintao's January 2011 commitments, 13 provinces had not yet issued any measures to comply.[106] In addition, an October 2012 USCBC survey found that 85% of respondents said they had seen little impact on their businesses resulting from China's commitments delinking indigenous innovation with government procurement.[107]

Remaining U.S. Concerns

While many U.S. business leaders have applauded China's pledge to delink indigenous innovation from government procurement, some remain wary that China will implement new policies that attempt to provide preferences to local Chinese firms over foreign firms. According to Adam Segal with the Council on Foreign Relations: "Even if China reverses certain policies under U.S. pressure, it will remain dedicated to those goals. U.S. policy is likely to become a game of Whac-a-Mole, beating down one Chinese initiative on indigenous innovation only to see another pop up."[108] U.S. business groups are also concerned with how the MLP blueprint will affect China's commitment to enforcing foreign IPR. They note, for example, that the MLP states: "Indigenous innovation refers to enhancing original innovation, integrated innovation, and re-innovation based on assimilation and absorption of imported technology, in order to improve our national innovation capability." To some, this seems to indicate that China intends to take existing technology, make some changes and improvements on it, and then claim it as its own without acknowledging or compensating the original IPR holders. A 2011 report by the U.S. Chamber of Commerce stated that China's indigenous innovation policies led many international technology companies to conclude that the MLP is a "blueprint for technology theft on a scale the world has never seen before."[109]

U.S. officials have attempted to convince Beijing that, while its desire to increase innovation in China is a commendable goal, its efforts to limit the participation of foreign firms in such efforts, or attempting to condition market access in China to the development of IPR by foreign firms in China will hinder, not promote, the advancement of innovation in China. The direction China takes on this issue could have a significant impact on U.S. economic interests as noted by a study by the U.S. International Trade Commission (USITC):

> To the extent that China's policies succeed in accelerating technological progress, productivity, and innovation in the Chinese economy, they could provide spillover benefits for other countries. But if indigenous innovation policies act as a form of technological import substitution, systematically favoring Chinese domestic firms over foreign firms in relevant industries, they would be expected to have a negative effect on foreign firms and economies roughly analogous to what would occur if China simply imposed a protective tariff on imports of goods in the relevant sectors or levied a discriminatory excise tax on the sales of FIEs in the Chinese market.[110]

Intellectual Property Rights (IPR)

U.S. business and government representatives have voiced growing concern over economic losses suffered by U.S. firms as a result of IPR infringement in China (and elsewhere), including those that have resulted from cyber-attacks. U.S. innovation and the intellectual property that is generated by such activities have been cited by various economists as a critical source of U.S. economic growth and global competitiveness.[111] For example, according to the Department of Commerce, in 2010, U.S. IP-intensive industries supported at least 40 million jobs and contributed $5.1 trillion (or 34.8%) to U.S. gross domestic product (GDP).[112] A study by NDP Consulting estimated that in 2008, workers in IP-intensive production earned 60% more than workers at similar levels in non-IP industries.[113] A study on the Apple iPod concluded that Apple's innovation in developing and engineering the iPod and its ability to source most of its production to low-cost countries, such as China, have helped enable it to become a highly competitive and profitable firm as well as a creator of high-paying jobs (such as engineers engaged in the design of Apple products) in the United States.[114]

Lack of effective and consistent protection of IPR has been cited by U.S. firms as one of the most significant problems they face in doing business in China. Other U.S. firms have expressed concern over pressures they often face from Chinese government entities to share technology and IPR with a Chinese partner. Although China has significantly improved its IPR protection regime over the past few years, U.S. IP industries complain that piracy rates in China continue to remain unacceptably high and economic losses are significant, as illustrated by studies and estimates made by several stakeholders:

- A May 2013 study by the Commission on the Theft of American Intellectual Property estimated the annual cost to the U.S. economy of global IPR theft at $300 billion, of which China accounted for 50% ($150 billion) to 80% ($240 billion) of those losses.[115]
- A 2013 AmCham China survey found that 72% of respondents said that China's IPR enforcement was either ineffective or totally ineffective.[116]
- The USITC estimated that U.S. intellectual property-intensive firms that conducted business in China lost $48.2 billion in sales, royalties, and license fees in 2009 because of IPR violations there. It also estimated that an effective IPR enforcement regime in China that was comparable to U.S. levels could increase employment by IP-intensive firms in the United States by 923,000 jobs.[117]
- The Business Software Alliance (BSA) estimated the commercial value of illegally used software in China at $8.9 billion in 2011 (up from $6.7 billion in 2007) and that the software piracy rate in China was 77% (down from 82% in 2007).[118] BSA further estimated that legitimate software sales in China were only $2.7 billion, compared to legal sales of $41.7 billion in the United States.
- The U.S. Customs and Border Protection reported that China accounted for 72% of pirated goods seized by the agency in FY2012 (based on domestic value). The value of seized goods originating from China and Hong Kong was $1.1 billion.[119] Handbags and wallets accounted for nearly half the estimated value of seized goods originating in China.

Chinese officials contend that they have significantly improved their IPR protection regime, but argue that the country lacks the resources and a sophisticated legal system to effectively deal with IPR violations. They also contend that IPR infringement is a serious problem for domestic Chinese firms as well. However, some analysts contend that China's relatively poor record on IPR enforcement can be partially explained by the fact that Chinese leaders want to make China a major producer of capital-intensive and high-technology products, and thus, they are tolerant of IPR piracy if it helps Chinese firms become more technologically advanced. According to an official at the U.S. Chamber of Commerce:

> The newer and emerging challenge to U.S. IPR is not a function of China's lack of political will to crackdown on infringers. Rather, it is a manifestation of a coherent, and government-directed, or at least government-motivated, strategy to lessen China's perceived reliance on foreign innovations and IP. China is actively working to create a legal environment that enables it to intervene in the market for IP, help its own companies to "re-innovate" competing IPR as a substitute to American and other foreign technologies, and potentially misappropriate U.S. and other foreign IP as components of its industrial policies and internal market regulation.... The common themes throughout these policies are: 1) undermine and displace foreign IP; 2) leverage China's large domestic market to develop national champions and promote its own IP, displacing foreign competitors in China; and 3)building on China's domestic successes by displacing competitors in foreign markets.[120]

An illustration of alleged IPR theft in China involves American Superconductor Corporation (AMSC). On September 14, 2011, AMSC announced that it was filing criminal and civil complaints in China against Sinovel Wind Group Co. Ltd. (Sinovel), China's largest wind turbine producer, and other parties, alleging the illegal use of AMSC's intellectual property. According to an AMSC press release, Sinovel illegally obtained and used AMSC's wind turbine control software code to upgrade its 1.5 megawatt wind turbines in the field to meet proposed Chinese grid codes and to potentially allow for the use of core electrical components from other manufacturers.[121] In addition, AMSC claimed that Sinovel had refused to pay for past shipments from AMSC and was now refusing to honor contracts for future shipments of components and spare parts as well.[122] AMSC has brought several civil cases against Sinovel, seeking to recover more than $1.2 billion for contracted shipments and damages caused by Sinovel's contract breaches.[123]

According to a specialist in intellectual property at Tufts University, "Chinese companies, once they acquire the needed technology, will often abandon their Western partners on the pretext the technology or product failed to meet Chinese governmental regulations. This is yet another example of a Chinese industrial policy aimed at procuring, by virtually any means, technology in order to provide Chinese domestic industries with a competitive advantage."[124]

During the December 2010 U.S.-China Joint Commission on Commerce and Trade (JCCT),[125] the Chinese government announced several new initiatives to improve its IPR protection regime, including boosting purchases of legitimate software by government agencies and 30 large SOEs. The USTR's 2011 *Special 301* report (an annual review of IPR and market access practices in foreign countries) noted that China had launched the "Program for Special Campaign on Combating IPR Infringement and Manufacture and Sales of Counterfeiting and Shoddy Commodities" (Special Campaign) in October 2010, aimed at a broad range of IPR violations. The Special Campaign involved 26 member agencies (led by a Chinese vice premier), and reportedly led to improved government coordination of IPR enforcement by the Chinese government.

The USTR's 2012 *Special 301* report stated that, while China had made some notable improvements to its IPR enforcement regime (in particular by making the Special Campaign on IPR enforcement permanent), serious problems remain. These include very high levels of trademark counterfeiting and copyright piracy, the persistence of "notorious" physical and online markets selling IPR-infringing goods, the manufacturing and sale of counterfeit pharmaceuticals, export of counterfeit goods, and discriminatory policies seeking to promote indigenous innovation in China by coercing foreign firms to transfer IPR to Chinese domestic firms. The USTR further noted a "recent alarming increase" in thefts of trade secrets (both in China and outside China) for the benefit of Chinese entities. Many of these problems, according to the USTR, stemmed from the lack of an effective government deterrent to such activities. In addition, while China's campaign to require central and provincial governments to use legitimate software produced a "modest increase" in U.S. software sales to the Chinese government, piracy rates by Chinese SOEs remained high.[126]

The USTR's 2013 Special 301 report stated that China had made comprehensive improvements to its trade laws and regulations, but indicated growing U.S. concern over the apparent growth of trade secret theft in China, including those involving departing employees, failed joint ventures, cyber intrusion and hacking (discussed in more detail below), and misuse of information submitted by U.S. firms to Chinese government entities for purposes of complying with regulatory obligations.[127] The USTR also noted that IPR enforcement remains a serious problem and has gotten worse because of cyber theft (discussed in more detail below). The USTR stated that the Chinese government viewed trade secret cases as routine commercial disputes, rather than as serious violations of the law. It further said that even though the Chinese government had reported that it had completed its plan to require the use of legitimate software by government entities at the central and provincial level, U.S. software firms had reported only a modest increase in sales to the government.

Market access in China remains a significant problem for many U.S. IP industries (such as music and films) and is considered to be a significant cause of high IPR piracy rates. For example, until recently, China limited imports of foreign films to 20 per year. During the visit to the United States by then-Chinese Vice President Xi Jinping (February 13-17, 2012), China agreed that it would allow more American exports to China of 3D, IMAX, and similar enhanced format movies on favorable commercial terms; strengthen the opportunities to distribute films through private enterprises rather than the state film monopoly; and ensure fairer compensation levels for U.S. blockbuster films distributed by Chinese SOEs.[128]

Technology Transfer Issues

When China entered the WTO in 2001, it agreed that foreign firms would not be pressured by government entities to transfer technology to a Chinese partner as part of the cost of doing business in China. However, many U.S. firms argue that this is a common Chinese practice, although this is difficult to quantify because, oftentimes, U.S. business representatives appear to try to avoid negative publicity regarding the difficulties they encounter doing business in China out of concern over retaliation by the Chinese government.[129]

In 2011, then-U.S. Treasury Secretary Timothy Geithner charged that "we're seeing China continue to be very, very aggressive in a strategy they started several decades ago, which goes like this: you want to sell to our country, we want you to come produce here. If you want to come produce here, you need to transfer your technology to us." A 2012 AmCham China survey reported that 33% of its respondents stated that technology transfer requirements were negatively affecting their businesses.[130] A 2010 study by the U.S. Chamber of Commerce stated that growing pressure on foreign firms to share technology in exchange for market access in China was forcing such firms to "anguish over balancing today's profits with tomorrow's survival."[131]

However, a 2011 survey by the USCBC found that technology transfer requirements by Chinese entities (both government and private) did not rank among the top 10 challenges faced by the Council's members in 2010. Among U.S. firms where technology was an issue, when asked if their company had been asked to transfer technology to China over the past three years, 18% answered yes. Among the respondents that had been asked to transfer technology, 20% said the pressure came from a government entity, while 80% said that it came from a Chinese company.[132] Of the respondents who said they were asked to transfer technology, 40% stated that they found the requests acceptable, 30% refused the requests, 15% negotiated to mitigate the amount of technology transfer, and 10% said they had to transfer the technology requested in order to gain access to the Chinese market. As noted by the USCBC:

> The PRC [People's Republic of China] certainty has a long-term strategy to bring in foreign technology. But technology is not simply "given to China." Instead, technology is typically licensed to a China-based entity in which the foreign company has an ownership stake. In many cases the foreign company owns 100 percent of the entity in China; in some cases, the foreign company must form a joint venture with a Chinese partner. In exchange, the company determines a value of the technology to be transferred and negotiates a payment— the technology is rarely "given" for free.[133]

Press reports indicate that the USTR's office is currently seeking information from U.S. manufacturers on examples of efforts by the Chinese government to force the transfer of technology from U.S. companies operating in China. This issue was discussed during President Obama's meeting with then-Chinese Vice President Xi Jinping on February 14, 2012.[134] A White House Factsheet of the meeting stated: "China reiterates that technology transfer and technological cooperation shall be decided by businesses independently and will not be used by the Chinese government as a pre-condition for market access."

In the 112th Congress, S. 2063 (Webb) would have prohibited the transfer by a U.S. commercial entity of any proprietary technology or intellectual property that was researched, developed, or commercialized using a contract, grant, loan, loan guarantee, or other financial assistance provided or awarded by the U.S. government to certain foreign entities (such as those that are owned or controlled by a foreign government) unless the Secretary of

Commerce determined (and issued a waiver) that the transfer would not compromise the U.S. economic interests or competitiveness.

Cyber Security Issues

Cyber-attacks against U.S. firms have raised concerns over the potential large-scale theft of U.S. IPR and its economic implications for the United States. A 2011 report by McAfee (a U.S. global security technology company) stated that its investigation had identified targeted intrusions into more than 70 global companies and warned that "every conceivable industry with significant size and valuable intellectual property has been compromised (or will be shortly), with the great majority of the victims rarely discovering the intrusion or its impact."[135] Many U.S. analysts and policy makers contend that the Chinese government is a major source of cyber-economic espionage against U.S. firms. For example, Representative Mike Rogers, chairman of the House Permanent Select Committee on Intelligence, stated at an October 4, 2011, hearing that

> Attributing this espionage isn't easy, but talk to any private sector cyber analyst, and they will tell you there is little doubt that this is a massive campaign being conducted by the Chinese government. I don't believe that there is a precedent in history for such a massive and sustained intelligence effort by a government to blatantly steal commercial data and intellectual property. China's economic espionage has reached an intolerable level and I believe that the United States and our allies in Europe and Asia have an obligation to confront Beijing and demand that they put a stop to this piracy.[136]

According to a report by the U.S. Office of the Director of National Intelligence (DNI): "Chinese actors are the world's most active and persistent perpetrators of economic espionage. U.S. private sector firms and cyber security specialists have reported an onslaught of computer network intrusions that have originated in China, but the IC (Intelligence Community) cannot confirm who was responsible." The report goes on to warn that

> China will continue to be driven by its longstanding policy of "catching up fast and surpassing" Western powers. The growing interrelationships between Chinese and U.S. companies—such as the employment of Chinese-national technical experts at U.S. facilities and the off-shoring of U.S. production and R&D to facilities in China—will offer Chinese government agencies and businesses increasing opportunities to collect sensitive US economic information.[137]

On February 19, 2013, Mandiant, a U.S. information security company, issued a report documenting extensive economic cyber espionage by a Chinese unit (which it designated as APT1) with alleged links to the Chinese People's Liberation Army (PLA) against 141 firms, covering 20 industries, since 2006. The report stated:

> Our analysis has led us to conclude that APT1 is likely government-sponsored and one of the most persistent of China's cyber threat actors. We believe that APT1 is able to wage such a long-running and extensive cyber espionage campaign in large part because it receives direct government support. In seeking to identify the organization behind this activity, our research found that People's Liberation Army (PLA's) Unit 61398 is similar to APT1 in its mission, capabilities, and resources. PLA Unit 61398 is also located in precisely the same area from which APT1 activity appears to originate.[138]

On March 11, 2013, Tom Donilon, National Security Advisor to President Obama, stated in a speech that the United States and China should engage in a constructive dialogue to establish acceptable norms of behavior in cyberspace; that China should recognize the urgency and scope of the problem and the risks it poses to U.S. trade relations and the reputation to Chinese industry; and that China should take serious steps to investigate and stop cyber espionage.[139] Following a meeting with Chinese President Xi Jinping in June 2013, President Obama warned that if cyber security issues are not addressed and if there continues to be direct theft of United States property, then "this was going to be a very difficult problem in the economic relationship and was going to be an inhibitor to the relationship really reaching its full potential."

On May 7, 2013, Senator Levin introduced S. 884, the Deter Cyber Theft Act. The bill would require the Director of National Intelligence (DNI) to develop a watch list and a priority watch list (determined to engage in the most egregious economic or industrial espionage in cyberspace) of foreign countries that engage in economic or industrial espionage in cyberspace with respect to U.S. trade secrets or proprietary information. The bill would require the president to block import of products containing stolen U.S. technology; products made by state-owned enterprises of nations on the DNI's priority watch list that are similar to items identified in the DNI's report as stolen or targeted U.S. technology; or made by a company the DNI identifies as having benefited from theft of U.S. technology or proprietary information.[140]

China's Obligations in the World Trade Organization

Negotiations for China's accession to the General Agreement on Tariffs and Trade (GATT) and its successor organization, the WTO, began in 1986 and took over 15 years to complete. During the WTO negotiations, Chinese officials insisted that China was a developing country and should be allowed to enter under fairly lenient terms. The United States insisted that China could enter the WTO only if it substantially liberalized its trade regime. In the end, a compromise was reached that required China to make immediate and extensive reductions in various trade and investment barriers, while allowing it to maintain some level of protection (or a transitional period of protection) for certain sensitive sectors. China's WTO membership was formally approved at the WTO Ministerial Conference in Doha, Qatar, on November 10, 2001. On November 11, 2001, China notified the WTO that it had formally ratified the WTO agreements, and on December 11, 2001, it formally joined the WTO.[141]

Under the WTO accession agreement, China agreed to the following.

- Reduce the average tariff for industrial goods from 17% to 8.9%, and average tariffs on U.S. priority agricultural products from 31% to 14%.
- Limit subsidies for agricultural production to 8.5% of the value of farm output, eliminate export subsidies on agricultural exports, and notify the WTO of all government subsidies on a regular basis.
- Within three years of accession, grant full trade and distribution rights to foreign enterprises (with some exceptions, such as for certain agricultural products, minerals, and fuels).
- Provide nondiscriminatory treatment to all WTO members, such as treating foreign firms in China no less favorably than Chinese firms for trade purposes.
- End discriminatory trade policies against foreign invested firms in China, such as domestic content rules and technology transfer requirements.
- Implement the WTO's Trade-Related Aspects of Intellectual Property Rights (TRIPS) Agreement upon accession (which sets basic standards on IPR protection and rules for enforcement).
- Fully open the banking system to foreign financial institutions within five years (by the end of 2006).
- Allow joint ventures in insurance and telecommunication (with various degrees of foreign ownership allowed).

WTO Implementation Issues

Getting China into the WTO under a comprehensive trade liberalization agreement was a major U.S. trade objective during the late 1990s. Many U.S. policy makers at the time maintained that China's WTO membership would encourage the Chinese government to deepen market reforms, promote the rule of law, reduce the government's role in the economy, further integrate China into the world economy, and enable the United States to use the WTO's dispute resolution mechanism to address major trade issues. As a result, it was hoped, China would become a more reliable and stable U.S. trading partner. U.S. trade officials contend that in the first years after it joined the WTO, China made noteworthy progress in adopting economic reforms that facilitated its transition toward a market economy and increased its openness to trade and FDI. However, beginning in 2006, progress toward further market liberalization appeared to slow. By 2008, U.S. government and business officials noted evidence of trends toward a more restrictive trade regime.[142] The USTR's 12th annual report to China on WTO compliance (issued in December 2013) identified several areas of concern, including[143]

- Failure by the Chinese government to maintain an effective IPR enforcement regime;
- Industrial policies and national standards that attempt to promote Chinese firms (while discriminating against foreign firms);
- Restrictions on trading and distribution rights;
- Discriminatory and unpredictable health and safety rules on imports (especially agricultural products);
- Burdensome regulations and restrictions on services; and
- Failure to provide adequate transparency of trade laws and regulations.

As of January 2014, the United States has brought 14 dispute settlement cases against China, 9 of which have been resolved or ruled upon.[144] China has nine WTO cases against the United States as well.[145] The U.S. cases are summarized below.

Pending U.S. WTO Dispute Settlement Cases Against China

- On September 17, 2012, the USTR announced that it had initiated a WTO dispute settlement case against China over it export subsidies to auto and auto parts manufacturers in China.[146]

- On March 13, 2012, the United States, Japan, and the European Union jointly initiated a dispute settlement case against China's restrictive export policies (such as quotas, tariffs, and minimum export prices) on rare earths and two other minerals.[147]
- On September 15, 2010, the USTR's office announced it was bringing a WTO case against China over its improper application of antidumping duties and countervailing duties on imports of grain oriented flat-rolled electrical steel from the United States. AWTO panel in June 2012 ruled largely in favor of the U.S. position and this was generally upheld by a WTO Appellate Body in October 2012. However, on December 24, 2013, the USTR stated that China had failed to bring its duties into compliance with WTO rules.

Resolved Cases or a WTO Panel Has Issued a Ruling[148]

- In May 2012, the United States initiated a WTO dispute settlement case China's improper use of anti-dumping and countervailing duties on broiler products. On August 5, 2013, the USTR announced that the United States had largely prevailed in the case.
- On September 15, 2010, the USTR's office announced it was bringing a WTO dispute settlement case against China over its discrimination against U.S. suppliers of electronic payment services (EPS). The United States charged that China permits only a Chinese entity (China Union Pay) to supply electronic payment services for payment card transactions denominated and paid in RMB in China, that service suppliers of other Members can only supply these services for payment card transactions paid in foreign currency, that China requires all payment card processing devices to be compatible with that entity's system and that payment cards must bear that company's logo, and that the Chinese entity has guaranteed access to all merchants in China that accept payment cards, while services suppliers of other WTO members must negotiate for access to merchants.[149] On July 16, 2012, the USTR announced that the United States had largely prevailed in the dispute.
- On June 23, 2009, the United States brought a case against China's export restrictions (such as export quotas and taxes) on raw materials (bauxite, coke, fluorspar, magnesium, manganese, silicon metal, silicon carbide, yellow phosphorus, and zinc). The United States charged that such policies are intended to lower prices for Chinese firms (steel, aluminum, and chemical sectors) in order to help them

obtain an unfair competitive advantage. China claims that these restraints are intended to conserve the environment and exhaustible natural resources. In July 2011, a WTO panel issued a report that China's export taxes and quotas on raw materials violated its WTO commitments. It further found that China failed to show that restrictions were linked to conservation of exhaustible natural resources for some of the raw materials or to protect the health of its citizens (by reducing pollution).[150] China appealed the WTO panel's ruling. However, on January 30, 2012, a WTO Appellate Body affirmed that China's export quotas and export taxes on certain raw materials violated its WTO commitments.[151] U.S. Trade Representative Ron Kirk called the decision a "tremendous victory for the United States," and said that it would ensure that "core manufacturing industries in this country can get the materials they need to produce and compete on a level playing field."[152]

- On December 22, 2010, the USTR's office announced that it would bring a WTO case against China over a government program that extended subsidies to Chinese wind power equipment manufacturers that use parts and components made in China rather than foreign-made parts and components. On June 7, 2011, the USTR's office announced that China had agreed to end these subsidies. However, the USTR noted that it had taken significant investigatory efforts by the U.S. government, working with industry and workers, to uncover China's wind subsidies because of the lack of transparency in China. The USTR further noted that, under the terms of China's WTO accession, it was required to fully report its subsidy programs to the WTO, which, to date, it has failed to do.[153]
- On December 19, 2008, the USTR filed a WTO case against China over its support for "Famous Chinese" brand programs, charging that such programs utilize various export subsidies (including cash grant rewards, preferential loans, research and development funding to develop new products, and payments to lower the cost of export credit insurance) at the central and local government level to promote the recognition and sale of Chinese brand products overseas. On December 18, 2009, the USTR announced that China had agreed to eliminate these programs.
- On March 3, 2008, the USTR requested WTO dispute resolution consultations with China regarding its discriminatory treatment of U.S. suppliers of financial information services in China. On

November 13, 2008, the USTR announced that China had agreed to eliminate discriminatory restrictions on how U.S. and other foreign suppliers of financial information services do business in China.

- On April 10, 2007, the USTR filed a WTO case against China, charging that it failed to comply with the TRIPS agreement (namely in terms of its enforcement of IPR laws). On January 26, 2009, the WTO ruled that many of China's IPR enforcement policies failed to fulfill its WTO obligations. On June 29, 2009, China announced that it would implement the WTO ruling by March 2010.
- On April 10, 2007, the USTR filed a WTO case against China charging that it failed to provide sufficient market access to IPR-related products, namely in terms of trading rights and distribution services. In August 2009, a WTO panel ruled that many of China's regulations on trading rights and distribution of films for theatrical release, DVDs, music, and books and journals were inconsistent with China's WTO obligation. China appealed the decision, but lost, and in February 2010 stated that it would implement the WTO's ruling.
- On February 5, 2007, the USTR announced it had requested WTO dispute consultations with China over government regulations that give illegal (WTO-inconsistent) import and export subsidies to various industries in China (such as steel, wood, and paper) that distort trade and discriminate against imports.[154] China's WTO accession agreement required it to immediately eliminate such subsidies. On November 29, 2007, China formally agreed to eliminate the subsidies in question by January 1, 2008.
- On March 30, 2006, the USTR initiated a WTO case against China over its use of discriminatory regulations on imported auto parts, which often applied the high tariff rate on finished autos (25%) to certain auto parts (which generally average 10%). The USTR charged that that the purpose of China's policy was to discourage domestic producers from using imported parts and to encourage foreign firms to move production to China. On February 13, 2008, a WTO panel ruled that China's discriminatory tariff policy was inconsistent with its WTO obligations (stating that the auto tariffs constituted an internal charge rather than ordinary customs duties, which violated WTO rules on national treatment). China appealed the decision, but a WTO Appellate Body largely upheld the WTO panel's decision.
- On March 18, 2004, the USTR announced it had filed a WTO dispute resolution case against China over its discriminatory tax treatment of

> imported semiconductors. The United States claimed that China applied a 17% value-added tax (VAT) on semiconductor chips that were designed and made outside China, but gave VAT rebates to domestic producers. Following consultations with the Chinese government, the USTR announced on July 8, 2004, that China agreed to end its preferential tax policy by April 2005. However, the USTR has expressed concern over new forms of financial assistance given by the Chinese government to its domestic semiconductor industry.

During his State of the Union Address in January 2012, President Obama announced plans to create a new Trade Enforcement Unit "charged with investigating unfair trade practices in countries like China." On February 28, 2012, President Obama issued an executive order establishing the Interagency Trade Enforcement Center within the USTR's office. Many analysts contend that the new enforcement unit could result in a sharp increase in the number of WTO dispute settlement cases brought by the United States against China.

China's Accession to the WTO Government Procurement Agreement (GPA)

Government procurement policies are largely exempt from WTO rules, except for those members which have signed the GPA.[155] When China joined the WTO, it indicated its intention to become a member of WTO's GPA as soon as possible, but, to date, has failed to submit an offer acceptable to current GPA members.

China's accession to the GPA is a major U.S. priority. China reports its annual government procurement spending at $179 billion (2011).[156] U.S. officials estimate this figure could be as high as $200 billion.[157] A study by the European Union Chamber of Commerce in China estimates that this figure could be well over $1 trillion if all levels of government are included, plus SOEs.[158] China currently maintains a number of restrictive government procurement practices and policies that favor domestic Chinese firms. Because of China's rapidly growing economy and significant infrastructure needs, China's accession to the GPA could result in significant new opportunities for U.S. firms.

China did not formally enter into negotiations to join the GPA until 2007, and its initial offer was deemed unacceptable by the other WTO GPA parties. China promised to revise its GPA offer, but did not do so until July 2010. That offer was deemed an improvement over the previous offer but was not accepted, in part because it excluded purchases by local and provincial governments as well as SOEs. A revised offer in December 2011 only covered public entities in three cities and two provinces.[159] Commenting on China's last offer, the USTR's office stated:

> China began its negotiations to join the GPA four years ago this month. Since that time, China has submitted three offers, each an improvement over the last. But China still has some distance to go before the procurement that it is offering is comparable to the extensive procurement that the United States and other Parties cover under the GPA. For example, we are urging China to cover state-owned enterprises, add more sub-central entities and services, reduce its thresholds for the size of covered contracts, and remove other broadexclusions.[160]

China submitted a new offer in November 2012. According to press reports, the U.S. representative to the WTO GPA committee stated that China's latest offer was "only another step but far from what we had expected." In particular, the United States and other GPA parties want China to improve its offer by including coverage of SOEs, lowering thresholds above which the GPA's nondiscrimination disciplines apply, removing several broad exclusions to coverage, and expanding coverage of sub-central entities. Some Members also stated opposition to China's proposal that it be allowed a five-year implementation period.[161] During the July 2013 S&ED talks, China pledged to submit a new revised GPA offer by the end of 2013 that would include lowering thresholds and increased coverage of sub-central entities.

Congressional concerns over China's restrictions on public procurement and failure to date to join the GPA resulted in the introduction of legislation in 112th Congress. H.R. 375 (Kildee) would have limited the total value of Chinese goods that could be procured by the U.S. government to the same value of U.S. goods procured by the Chinese government in the previous year, while H.R. 2271 (Royce) would have prohibited the federal government from awarding contracts to Chinese entities until China signs the GPA.

China's Currency Policy[162]

Unlike most advanced economies (such as the United States), China does not maintain a market-based floating exchange rate. Between 1994 and July 2005, China pegged its currency, the renminbi (RMB) or yuan, to the U.S. dollar at about 8.28 yuan to the dollar.[163] In July 2005, China appreciated the RMB to the dollar by 2.1% and moved to a "managed float," based on a basket of major foreign currencies, including the U.S. dollar. In order to maintain a target rate of exchange with the dollar (and other currencies), the Chinese government has maintained restrictions and controls over capital transactions and has made large-scale purchases of U.S. dollars (and dollar assets).[164] According to the Bank of China, from July 2005 to July 2009, the official exchange rate went from 8.27 to 6.83 yuan per dollar, an appreciation of 21.1%.[165] However, once the effects of the global financial crisis became apparent, the Chinese government halted its appreciation of the RMB and subsequently kept the yuan/dollar exchange rate relatively constant at 6.83 from July 2009 to June 2010 in order to help limit the impact of the sharp decline in global demand for Chinese products. From June 19, 2010, (when appreciation was resumed) to December 17, 2013, the yuan/dollar exchange rate went from 6.83 to 6.11, an appreciation of 11.8%. Most of the appreciation occurred in 2010 and 2011. From January 1, 2012, to December 17, 2013, the RMB appreciated by only 3.6% against the dollar. Some analysts maintain that this is an indicator that the Chinese government is continuing to heavily intervene in currency markets to hold the down value of RMB relatively constant in the face of weak global demand for Chinese exports. Others argue that market forces are the main cause of the slow appreciation of the RMB, noting that China's current account surplus and accumulation of foreign exchange reserves have slowed considerably over the past few years which, it is argued, have lessened the need for the Chinese government to intervene in currency markets.

Many U.S. policy makers, labor groups, and business representatives of import-sensitive industries have charged that China's currency remains significantly undervalued against the dollar. They claim that this policy provides an indirect subsidy to Chinese exporters (which makes Chinese goods less expensive in the United States), while acting as a de facto tariff on U.S. goods imported into China (which makes them more expensive). They argue that this policy has particularly hurt several U.S. manufacturing sectors that are forced to compete against low-cost Chinese products and has led to significant job losses in the United States, especially in manufacturing. Critics further charge that China's currency policy has been a major factor in the size and growth of the U.S. trade deficit with China. Some Members of Congress contend that, given the current high rate of unemployment in the United States, Chinese "currency manipulation" can no longer be tolerated.

U.S. officials have urged China to continue efforts to rebalance its economy by boosting consumer demand (which would increase import demand) and decreasing the reliance on exports and fixed investment for economic growth. They argue that doing so would enable the Chinese government to move more quickly toward adopting a market-based exchange rate since the creation of new jobs in the nontrade sector would offset job losses in the trade sector resulting from an appreciation of the RMB.

Numerous bills have been introduced in Congress over the past few years that would seek to induce China to reform its currency policy or would attempt to address the perceived effects that policy has on the U.S. economy. For example, one bill in the 108th Congress would have imposed an additional duty of 27.5% on imported Chinese products unless China appreciated its currency to near market levels. In the 111th Congress, the House passed an amended version of H.R. 2378 (Tim Ryan), which would have made certain misaligned currencies (such as the RMB) actionable under U.S. countervailing duty cases on foreign government export subsidies (although the Senate did not take up the bill). In the 112th Congress, the Senate passed S. 1619, which would have provided for the identification of fundamentally misaligned currencies and required action to correct the misalignment for certain "priority" countries.

Two currency bills have been introduced in the 113th Congress: H.R. 1276 and S. 1114. H.R. 1276, the Currency Reform for Fair Trade Act was introduced by Representative Sander Levin on March 20, 2013. The bill is identical to the one he introduced in the 112th Congress (H.R. 639) and nearly identical to H.R. 2378, which passed the House during the 111th Congress by a vote of 284 to 123. The bill would seek to clarify certain provisions of U.S. countervailing duty laws (pertaining to foreign government export subsidies) that would allow the Commerce Department to consider a "fundamentally misaligned currency" as an actionable subsidy. S. 1114, the Currency Exchange Rate Oversight Reform Act of 2013, was introduced by Senator Sherrod Brown on June 7, 2013, and is essentially the same bill he introduced in 2011 and was passed by the Senate on October 11, 2011. The bill would provide for the identification of fundamentally misaligned currencies and require action to correct the misalignment for certain "priority" countries.

Some Members have expressed opposition to various currency bills aimed at China, arguing that they could violate U.S. obligations in the WTO. Other Members have argued that, while inducing China to adopt a market-based exchange rate is an important goal, the United States should give higher priority to addressing China's industrial policies and IPR infringement, which some view as more damaging to U.S. economic interests.

THE U.S.-CHINA STRATEGIC AND ECONOMIC DIALOGUE

On September 29, 2006, President George W. Bush and Chinese President Hu Jintao agreed to establish a Strategic Economic Dialogue (SED) to have discussions on major economic issues at the "highest official level." According to a U.S. Treasury Department press release, the intent of the SED was to "discuss long-term strategic challenges, rather than seeking immediate solutions to the issues of the day," in order to provide a stronger foundation for pursuing concrete results through existing bilateral economic dialogues.[166] The first meeting was held in December 2006. Four subsequent rounds of talks were held (the last was in December 2008).

While attending the G-20 summit in London on the global financial crisis on April 1, 2009, President Obama and Chinese President Hu agreed to continue the high-level forum, renaming it the U.S.-China Strategic and Economic Dialogue (S&ED). The new dialogue is based on two tracks. The first (the "Strategic Track") is headed by the Secretary of State on the U.S. side and focuses on political and strategic issues, while the second track (the "Economic Track") is headed by the U.S. Treasury Secretary on the U.S. side and focuses on financial and economic issues. Areas of discussion include economic and trade issues, counterterrorism, law enforcement, science and technology, education, culture, health, energy, the environment (including climate change), nonproliferation, and human rights.

One of the reported benefits of the U.S-China S&ED process is that it brings together top economic officials from both sides (as well as U.S. Cabinet officials and Chinese heads of ministries) on a regular basis, which enables both sides to identify their major positions and priorities on various issues and to develop long-term working relationships. Some in Congress have criticized the S&ED forum, arguing that it produces few concrete results, and that many of the results described in subsequent fact sheets that are jointly issued simply restate agreements or pledges China has already made. Others counter that U.S. engagement with China occurs on multiple levels throughout the year and that the S&ED meetings are in part a cumulative result of this process.

The July 2009 Economic Track Session

The first round of the S&ED was held in Washington, DC, on July 27-28, 2009, and involved 12 U.S. Cabinet officials and agency heads and 15 Chinese ministers, vice ministers, and agency heads. The session was focused heavily on issues relating to the global economic crisis. Then-Secretary of the Treasury Timothy Geithner stated: "Recognizing that cooperation between China and the United States will remain vital not only to the well-being of our two nations but also the health of the global economy, we agreed to undertake policies to bring about sustainable, balanced global growth once economic recovery is firmly in place."

The two sides agreed to establish a framework of cooperation based on four pillars:

- Advancing macroeconomic and structural policies to achieve sustainable and balanced growth;
- Promoting more resilient, open, and market-oriented financial systems;
- Strengthening trade and investment ties; and
- Strengthening the international financial architecture.

These pillars appear to have been aimed at deepening bilateral cooperation in response to the global economic crisis, continuing commitments on both sides to promote policies that seek to achieve more balanced economic growth, encouraging China to continue economic and financial reforms, expanding China's role and/or participation in international economic forums,[167] and attempting to avoid new forms of trade protection.

May 2010 Economic Track Session

The May 24-25, 2010, S&ED economic session focused heavily on the continuing efforts relating to the four pillars identified in the July 2009 session. Although few concrete accomplishments were announced at the end of the meetings, the two agreed to intensify talks on a number of bilateral economic and trade issues. The two sides pledged to

- Sign a cooperation protocol on small and medium-sized firms (SMEs);
- Boost economic cooperation at the central and local government level, such as promoting the establishment of state-to-province and city-to-city partnerships;
- Conduct "intensive expert and high-level discussions" as early as the summer of 2010 on innovation issues (such as China's indigenous

innovation proposals) and take into account the results of these talks in formulating and implementing their innovation measures;[168]

- Improve cooperation to address health and safety issues relating to U.S. sales of soybeans to China;
- Establish a cooperative mechanism between the U.S. Export-Import Bank and the Export-Import Bank of China on trade finance, and develop initiatives to promote exports by SMEs;
- Explore the possibility of cooperating to enable the United States to treat China as a market economy, and treat certain Chinese firms as market-oriented industries, for the purpose of U.S. trade remedy laws; and
- Boost investment opportunities and transparency.[169]

The May 2011 Economic Track

The third round of the S&ED was held in Washington, DC, on May 9-10, 2011. Prior to the meeting, U.S. officials identified several goals for the economic track of the S&ED, including ensuring that China followed through on previous economic and trade commitments (such as on IPR protection and indigenous innovation policies) and encouraging China to make a number of reforms to its financial sector (such as adopting market-based interest rates on bank deposits and expanding market access in China for U.S. financial firms). China pledged to continue to promote domestic consumption, improve IPR enforcement, eliminate all of its indigenous innovation products catalogues, improve transparency of its economic and trade policies, and provide significant new opportunities for U.S. financial services firms in China.

The May 2012 Economic Track

The fourth S&ED round was held in Beijing on May 3 and 4, 2012, and focused largely on economic rebalancing and boosting foreign access to China's financial services sector.[170] China pledged that it would:

- Increase the number of SOEs that pay dividends;
- Participate in negotiations (beginning in the summer of 2012) for new rules on official export financing with the United States and other major exporters;

- Provide nondiscriminatory treatment to all enterprises, regardless of type of ownership, in terms of credit, taxation, and regulatory policies so that U.S. firms can more easily compete against Chinese SOEs;
- Submit a new robust offer in 2012 to join the WTO's GPA and to intensify efforts to negotiate a BIT with the United States;
- Open up more sectors to FDI and improve the transparency of its investment approval process;
- Prioritize the protection of trade secrets, extend efforts to promote the use of legal software by Chinese enterprises, treat IPR owned or developed in other countries the same as IPR owned or developed in China, and hold discussions with U.S. officials on the implementation of China's commitment not to make technology transfer a pre-condition for doing business in China;
- Take steps to raise household income and lower prices of consumer goods, such as cutting import tariffs, reducing taxes on services, and raising deposit rates; and
- Expand market access to domestic financial markets by boosting the permitted level of foreign investment in its stock and bond markets, raising the permitted foreign equity stake in domestic securities joint ventures from 33% to 49%, and allowing foreign investors to establish joint venture brokerages to trade commodity and financial futures (with up to a 49% equity stake).

The May 2013 Economic Track

The 5th round of the S&ED talks were held in Washington, DC, on July 10-11, 2013. China pledged that it would:

- Negotiate a high-standard bilateral investment treaty with the United States that would include all stages of investment and all sectors based on a negative list approach;
- Submit a new and improved offer to join the WTO GPA by the end of 2013 that would include lowered thresholds and increased coverage of sub-central entities;
- Establish a pilot Free Trade Zone program in Shanghai which would enable foreign enterprises to compete on the same terms as Chinese firms across a wide range of services sectors;

- Affirmed its support for concluding negotiations by 2014 for new comprehensive international agreement setting guidelines on export financing by the major providers of export credits that would be consistent with international best practices;
- Eliminate preferential input pricing for energy, land, and water given to SOEs and develop a market-based mechanism for determining;
- Strengthening financial regulatory cooperation; and
- Continue to implement polices to boost private consumption such as raising social security and employment spending by two percentage points of total fiscal spending by the end of 2015.

Some analysts have argued that the S&ED structure should be reformed. For example, a report by the Center for Strategic and International Studies (CSIS) argues that ceremony has come to overwhelm substance in the S&ED, that pressure for short-term deliverables at each event has detracted from the dialogue's objective of fostering long-term strategic cooperation, and that the structure of the S&ED has undermined the efforts of individual agencies to work on critical elements of the relationship.[171] Others have complained about the lack of benchmarks in the S&ED process to evaluate outcomes of China's commitments. Others complain that the S&ED process often fails to achieve results on major issues. For example, at the July 2013 S&ED, China made no specific commitment on halting cyber theft.

Concluding Observations

China's rapid economic growth and emergence as a major economic power have given China's leadership increased confidence in its economic model. The key challenges for the United States are to convince China that (1) it has a stake in maintaining the international trading system, which is largely responsible for its economic rise, and to take a more active leadership role in maintaining that system; and (2) further economic and trade reforms are the surest way for China to expand and modernize its economy. For example, by boosting domestic spending and allowing its currency to appreciate, China would likely import more, which would help speed economic recovery in other countries, promote more stable and balanced economic growth in China, and lessen trade protectionist pressures around the world. Improving IPR protection in China and providing nondiscriminatory treatment to foreign IP firms would likely foster greater innovation in China and attract more FDI in high technology than has occurred under current policies. Lowering trade barriers on imports would increase competition in China, lower costs for consumers, and boost economic efficiency. Some observers contend that reformist-minded officials in China will continue to push for greater free-market reforms, while others argue that vested interests in China (such as SOEs and export-oriented firms) who benefit from the status-quo will make further economic reforms more difficult to realize.

There are a number of views in the United States over how to more effectively address commercial disputes with China:

- Take a more aggressive stand against China, such as increasing the number of dispute settlement cases brought against China in the WTO, threatening to impose trade sanctions against China unless it addresses policies (such as IPR theft) that hurt U.S. economic interests, and making greater use of U.S. trade remedy laws (such as anti-dumping and countervailing measures) to address China's "unfair" trade practices.
- Intensify negotiations through existing high-level bilateral dialogues, such as the U.S.-China S&ED, which was established to discuss long-term challenges in the relationship. In addition, seek to complete ongoing U.S. negotiations with China to reach a high-standard BIT, as well as to finalize negotiations in the WTO toward achieving China's accession to the GPA. Continue to encourage China to implement comprehensive economic reforms, such as diminishing the role of the state in the economy and implementing policies to boost domestic consumption.
- Encourage China to join the Trans-Pacific Partnership (TPP) negotiations and/or seek to negotiate a bilateral a free trade agreement (FTA) with China that would require it to significantly improve IPR protection, lower trade and FDI barriers, and adopt new disciplines on the treatment of SOEs.[172]

End Notes

[1] This report focuses primarily on U.S.-China trade relations. For information on China's economy, see CRS Report RL33534, *China's Economic Rise: History, Trends, Challenges, and Implications for the United States*, by Wayne M. Morrison. For general information on U.S.-China political ties, see CRS Report R41108, *U.S.-China Relations: An Overview of Policy Issues*, by Susan V. Lawrence.

[2] The United States suspended China's MFN status in 1951, which cut off most bilateral trade. China's MFN status was conditionally restored in 1980 under the provisions set forth under Title IV of the 1974 Trade Act, as amended (including the Jackson-Vanik freedom-of-emigration provisions). China's MFN status (which was re-designated under U.S. trade law as "normal trade relations" status, or NTR) was renewed on an annual basis until January 2002, when permanent NTR was extended to China (after it joined the WTO in December 2001).

[3] U.S.-China Business Council, *China's WTO Compliance*, September 20, 2013.

[4] *OECD/WTO Trade in value-Added (TIVA) Database: China*, at http://www.oecd.org/sti/ind/TiVA%20China.pdf.

[5] U.S. Bureau of Economic Analysis, *U.S. International Services*.

[6] China's real GDP growth from 2008 to 2012 averaged 9.2%.

[7] Boston Consulting Group, *Big Prizes in Small Places: China's Rapidly Multiplying Pockets of Growth,* November 2010, p. 10.

[8] Boston Consulting Group, *Global Wealth 2013: Maintaining Momentum in a Complex World*, May 30, 2013.

[9] Source: *Economist Intelligence Unit.*

[10] China Daily, "China to invest 7t Yuan for Urban Infrastructure in 2011-15," May 13, 2013.

[11] China Daily, "China's Mobile Phone Users Hit 1.22 Billion," November 21, 2013.

[12] Boeing Corporation, *Current Market Outlook: 2013-2032*, September 5, 2013, available at http://www.boeing.com/assets/pdf/commercial/cmo/pdf/Boeing_Current_Market_Outlook_2013.pdf.

[13] Internet World Stats, at http://www.internetworldstats.com/stats.htm.

[14] A large share of these vehicles was produced by GM and its joint-venture partners in China. According to GM's website, it currently has 12 joint ventures and two wholly owned foreign enterprises in China and employees more than 58,000 workers. See, https://media.gm.com/media/cn/en/gm/company.html.

[15] BEA, *U.S. International Services*.

[16] Pacific Rim countries include Australia, Brunei, Cambodia, China, Hong Kong, Indonesia, Japan, South Korea, Laos, Macao, Malaysia, New Zealand, North Korea, Papua New Guinea, the Philippines, Singapore, Taiwan, Thailand, Vietnam, and several small island nations.

[17] China's accession to the WTO (with the reduction of trade and investment barriers) appears to have been a major factor behind the migration of computer production from other countries to China.

[18] USITC, *How Much of Chinese Exports Is Really Made In China? Assessing Foreign and Domestic Value-Added in Gross Exports*, report number 2008-03-B, March 2008, p. 21.

[19] Communications of the ACM, *Who Captures Value in a Global Innovation Network? The Case of Apple's iPod*, March 2009.

[20] U.S. data on FDI flows to and from China differ from Chinese data on FDI flows to and from the United States. This section examines only U.S. data.

[21] Investment is often a major factor behind trade flows. Firms that invest overseas often import machinery, parts, and other inputs from the parent company to manufacture products for export or sale locally. Other such invested overseas firms may produce inputs and ship them to their parent company for final production.

[22] 15 CFRS 806.15(a)(1). The 10% ownership share is the threshold considered to represent an effective voice or lasting influence in the management of an enterprise. See BEA, *International Economic Accounts, BEA Series Definitions*, available at http://www.bea.gov/international.

[23] BEA also reports FDI data according to broad industrial sections, including mining; utilities; wholesale trade; information; depository institutions; finance (excluding depository institutions); professional, scientific, and technical services; nonbank holding companies; manufacturing (including food, chemicals, primary and fabricated metals, machinery,

computers and electronic products, electrical equipment, appliances and components, transportation equipment, and other manufacturing); and other industries.

[24] For additional information on this issue, see CRS Report RL34314, *China's Holdings of U.S. Securities: Implications for the U.S. Economy*, by Wayne M. Morrison and Marc Labonte.

[25] The Treasury Department estimates that 72% of China's total holdings of U.S. government and private securities as of June 2012 were in U.S. Treasury securities.

[26] China's large annual trade surpluses and inflows of FDI are major contributors to China's accumulation of foreign exchange reserves, which totaled $3.4 trillion as of March 2013.

[27] However, over the past years, Chinese officials have expressed concern over the "safety" of their large holdings of U.S. debt. They worry that growing U.S. government debt and expansive monetary policies will eventually spark inflation in the United States, resulting in a sharp depreciation of the dollar. This would diminish the value of China's dollar asset holdings.[27] Some Chinese officials have called for replacing the dollar as the world's major reserve currency with some other currency arrangement, such as through the International Monetary Fund's special drawing rights system, although many economists question whether this would be a feasible alternative in the short run.

[28] China's holdings as of June 2012 were down $135 billion over June 2011 levels. In June 2012, Japan overtook China as the largest holder of U.S. public and private securities.

[29] Some observers characterize foreign holdings of U.S. Treasury securities as "foreign ownership of U.S. government debt."

[30] Office of the Secretary of Defense, *Report to Congress, Assessment of the National Security Risks Posed to the United States as a Result of the U.S. Federal Debt Owed to China as a Creditor of the U.S. Government*, July 2012.

[31] Note, U.S. and Chinese data on FDI flows between each other differ.

[32] According the BEA, direct investment implies that a person in one country has a lasting interest in, and a degree of influence over the management of, a business enterprise in another. As such, it defines FDI as ownership or control of 10% or more of an enterprise's voting securities, or the equivalent, is considered evidence of such a lasting interest or degree of influence over management.

[33] Chinese data lists the United States as the fourth-largest overall source of cumulative FDI through 2012. Chinese data on FDI flows with the United States differ from U.S. data.

[34] BEA data indicate that a significant cause of the decline in the stock of U.S. FDI in China over the past two years was from a decrease in the stock of U.S. FDI in depository institutions in China.

[35] BEA, U.S. *Direct Investment Abroad: Financial and Operating Data for U.S. Multinational Companies*, available at http://www.bea.gov/international/di1usdop.htm.

[36] Rhodium Group, *China Investment Monitor, Tracking Chinese Direct Investment in the U.S.* at http://rhgroup.net/ interactive/china-investment-monitor.

[37] Suntech press release, March 12, 2013, available at http://ir.suntech-power.com/phoenix.zhtml?c=192654&p=irol-newsArticle&id=1794801.

[38] Sany America website at http://www.sanyamerica.com/about-sany-america.php#ribbon.

[39] *Washington Post*, "Job creation seen as key to China's investment in U.S," January 19, 2011,available at http://www.washingtonpost.com/wp-dyn/content/article/2011/01/18/AR2011011806676.html.

[40] The purchase reportedly represents China's biggest single investment in the global auto parts-making industry and will make the Chinese company the largest private employer in Saginaw, Michigan at nearly 3,000 (source: New York Times, *G.M. Sells Parts Maker to a Chinese Company,* November 29, 2010). The firm owns 20 manufacturing plants worldwide, 5 regional engineering and test centers, and 14 local customer support centers.

[41] Xinhua News Agency, "U.S official hails Chinese Project in Texas, October 11, 2011."

[42] http://www.prnewswire.com/news-releases/huawei-poised-to-sustain-tens-of-thousands-of-job-opportunities-for-us-businesses-139525078.html.

[43] U.S. Department of the Treasury, *Preliminary Report on Foreign Portfolio Holdings of U.S. Securities at End-June 2011*, February, 29, 2012.

[44] For more information on the CIC, see CRS Report R41441, *China's Sovereign Wealth Fund: Developments and Policy Implications*, by Michael F. Martin.

[45] According to the BEA, Chinese majority-owned nonbank affiliates in the United States employed 1,700 U.S. workers in 2006 (most recent data available).

[46] During the 1980s, Japanese firms significantly boosted their FDI in the United States, such as in automobile manufacturing, in part to help to alleviate bilateral trade tensions.

[47] According to the United Nation's Conference on Trade and Development, China became the third-largest source of FDI outflows in 2012 at $84 billion (up from being the sixth largest in 2011).

[48] The White House, *Joint Fact Sheet on Strengthening U.S.-China Economic Relations*, February 14, 2012.

[49] CFIUS is an interagency committee that serves the President in overseeing the national security implications of foreign investment in the U.S. economy. See CRS Report RL33388, *The Committee on Foreign Investment in the United States (CFIUS)*, by James K. Jackson.

[50] Some argued, for example, that, given the relatively poor food safety record of many Chinese firms in China, the acquisition of Smithfield by Chinese investors could undermine food safety in the United States, and some suggested that the acquisition would eventually result in Chinese pork exports to the United States.

[51] The text of the letter can be found at http://www.stabenow.senate.gov/?p=press_release&id=1061.

[52] Senate Committee on Agriculture, Nutrition, and Forestry, available at http://www.ag.senate.gov/hearings/smithfield-and-beyond.

[53] The text of the letter can be found at http://www.finance.senate.gov/newsroom/chairman/release/?id=22b5b74e-5477-4ff8-9346-b46e0e158738.

[54] The letter is available at http://delauro.house.gov/index.php?option=com_content&view=article&id=1328:delauro-warren-demand-answers-on-shuanghui-smithfield-foods-deal&catid=2:2012-press-releases&Itemid=21.

[55] A123 Systems, Press Release, January 29, 2013, available at http://www.a123systems.com/62ce67cf-68aa-4b23-8b12-b8b210af1a3c/media-room-2013-press-releases-detail.htm.

[56] Investigative Report on the U.S. National Security Issues Posed by Chinese Telecommunications Companies Huawei and ZTE, A Report by Chairman Mike Rogers and Ranking Member C.A. Dutch Ruppersberger of the Permanent Select Committee on Intelligence, October 22, 2012, available at http://intelligence.house.gov/sites/intelligence.house.gov/files/documents/Huawei-ZTE%20Investigative%20Report%20(FINAL).pdf.

[57] New York Times, *Obama Orders Chinese Company to End Investment at Sites Near Drone Base*, September 28, 2012. Available at http://www.nytimes.com/2012/09/29/us/politics/chinese-company-ordered-to-give-up-stake-in-wind-farms-near-navy-base.html.

[58] Senator Robert Casey, *Press Release*, May 10, 2012, available at http://www.federalreserve.gov.

[59] The letter is available at http://www.casey.senate.gov/newsroom/press/release/?id=b940fb00-0a69-42d6-bcff-6ac72c8ce0c1.

[60] The letter also raised concerns over allegations that Huawei had ties to the Iranian government, had received substantial subsidies from the Chinese government, and had a poor record of protecting intellectual property rights.

[61] Huawei initially stated that it would decline CFIUS's recommendation with the intent of going through all of the procedures of the CFIUS process (including a potential decision by the President) in order to "reveal the truth about Huawei."

[62] Huawei, Open Letter, February 25, 2011, available at http://www.huawei.com/huawei_open_letter.do.

[63] A press release by Ansteel stated that its intensions are "to capitalize on the opportunity to enter into an overseas joint venture with a company that is focused on utilizing advanced

technology in an environmentally friendly and highly profitable manner." See, http://www.steeldevelopment.com/documents/ansteel2010.pdf.

[64] See letter at http://visclosky.house.gov/SC_Geithner_CFIUS_7.2.10.pdf.

[65] Testimony of Rep. Peter J. Visclosky before the U.S.-China Economic and Security Review Commission on China's State-Owned and State-Controlled Enterprises, February 15, 2012.

[66] Emcore Press Release, June 28, 2010, available at http://www.emcore.com/news_events/release?y=2010&news=249.

[67] *New York Times*, "Chinese Withdraw Offer for Nevada Gold Concern," December 21, 2009.

[68] Although Huawei states that it is a private company wholly owned by its employees, many analysts contend that the company has close connections to the Chinese military. In addition, Huawei has also reportedly received extensive financial support from the Chinese government, including a $30 billion line of credit from China Development Bank.

[69] The Senate report of its version of FINSA (S.Rept. 110-80, S. 1610) noted that CNOOC's attempt to acquire UNOCAL "led many members of Congress to raise questions about the transfer of ownership or control of certain sectors of the U.S. economy to foreign companies, especially to foreign companies located within or controlled by countries the governments of which might not be sympathetic to U.S. regional security interests."

[70] IBM and Lenovo reportedly agreed to address national security concerns by CFIUS. For example, it was agreed that 1,900 employees from a North Carolina research facility, which IBM had shared with other technology companies, would move to another building. See the *Financial Times*, "US State Department limits use of Chinese PCs," May 18, 2006.

[71] U.S.-China Business Council, China's WTO Compliance, September 20, 2013.

[72] OECD, FDI Regulatory Restrictiveness Index, at http://www.oecd.org/investment/fdiindex.htm.

[73] The automotive industry was designated a "pillar industry" by the Chinese government in 1991.

[74] China also maintains a permitted category which represents a neutral position by the government that FDI in that area is neither encouraged nor discouraged. Prior to 2012, FDI in the manufacture of complete automobiles was listed as an encouraged category, but now is listed under the neutral category.

[75] One major function of the Guideline Catalogue for Foreign Investment is to promote FDI in sectors that the government has targeted for growth in its five-year macro-economic plans.

[76] USTR, 2011 *Report to Congress on China's WTO Compliance*, December 2011, p. 7.

[77] AmCham *China, China Business Climate Survey*, 2013, p. 9.

[78] For example, in March 2011, Senators Casey, Schumer, Stabenow, and Whitehouse sent a letter to the Obama Administration urging that they oppose Chinese mining projects in the United States because of China's restrictive and anticompetitive policies on rare earth. The letter noted China's prohibition on foreign investment in rare earth mining and requirements that FDI in rare earth smelting and separation can only be in the form of a joint venture. See http://www.casey.senate.gov/newsroom/press/release/print.cfm?id=81a1fa95-49d2-47a7-98b4-65973ae14ddc.

[79] *Inside U.S.-China Trade*, April 28, 2010.

[80] The Administration began efforts to review and revise the U.S. BIT model in 2009. The previous BIT model dated to 2004. The Administration's review process likely meant that negotiations with China for a BIT were someone limited.

[81] U.S. Department of the Treasury, *Remarks of Treasury Secretary Jacob J. Lew at the Close of the Fifth U.S.-China Strategic and Economic Dialogue*, July 13, 2013.

[82] The impact of globalization has been a controversial topic in the United States. Some argue that it has made it easier for U.S. firms to shift production overseas, resulting in lost jobs in the United States (especially in manufacturing) and lower wages for U.S. workers. Others contend that globalization has induced U.S. firms to become more efficient and to focus a greater share of their domestic manufacturing on higher-end or more technologically advanced production (while sourcing lower-end production abroad), making such firms

more globally competitive. The result has been that the United States continues to be a major global manufacturer in terms of value-added, but there are fewer U.S. workers in manufacturing.

[83] World Trade Organization, *Trade Policy Review Body, Trade Policy Review, Report by the Secretariat, China*, Revision, 2010, Part 2, p. 1.

[84] U.S. Trade Representative, *2013 USTR Report to Congress on China's WTO Compliance*, December 2013, p. 2.

[85] U.S.-China Economic and Security Review Commission, *An Analysis of State-owned Enterprises and State Capitalism in China,* by Andrew Szamosszegi and Cole Kyle, October 26, 2011, p.1.

[86] *Xinhua Agency*, October 24, 2012.

[87] Xinhua News Agency, October 24, 2010.

[88] Testimony for the U.S.–China Economic and Security Review Commission by Derek Scissors, Ph.D, *Chinese State Owned Enterprises and the US Policy on China*, February 12, 2012.

[89] Anderson, G.E., PhD, *Designated Drivers, How China Plans to Dominate the Global Auto Industry*, 2012, p. 2.

[90] Lund University, *Lending for Growth? An Analysis of State-Owned Banks in China*, by Fredrik N.G. Anderson, Katarzyna Burzynska, and Sonja Opper, June 2013, p. 41.

[91] The Economist, *State Capitalism's Global Reach, New Masters of the Universe, How State Enterprise is Spreading*, January 21, 2012.

[92] Lund University, *Lending for Growth? An Analysis of State-Owned Banks in China*, by Fredrik N.G. Anderson, Katarzyna Burzynska, and Sonja Opper, June 2013, p. 41.

[93] McGregor, Richard, *The Party, the Secret World of China's Communist Rulers*, 2010, p. 204.

[94] As some observers describe it, China wants to go from a model of "made in China" to "innovated in China."

[95] The MLP identifies main areas and priority topics, including energy, water and mineral resources, the environment, agriculture, manufacturing, communications and transport, information industry and modern service industries, population and health, urbanization and urban development, public security, and national defense. The report also identifies 16 major special projects and 8 "pioneer technologies."

[96] *R&D Magazine*, December 22, 2009.

[97] U.S. business representatives also claim that the Chinese government is using tax incentives, standards setting and requirements, security regulations, subsidies, technology transfer requirements, and other measures to promote the goals of indigenous innovation.

[98] AmCham China, *2011 White Paper*, April 26, 2011, p. 66.

[99] A copy of the letter can be found at http://online.wsj.com/public/resources/documents/chinaprocurementletter1210.pdf.

[100] Some U.S. business representatives argue that one of the main goals of China's indigenous innovation regulations is to induce foreign firms to boost their R&D activities in China in order to qualify for government contracts.

[101] Transitional Review Under Section 18 of the Protocol on the Accession of the People's Republic of China, Report to the General Council by the Chair, November 17, 2011, p. 4.

[102] Wall Street Journal, *China Defends Rule On 'Indigenous' Tech*, December 15, 2009.

[103] The White House, *U.S. - China Joint Statement*, January 19, 2011.

[104] According to a U.S. fact sheet on the meeting "China pledged to eliminate all of its government procurement indigenous innovation products catalogues and revise Article 9 of the draft Government Procurement Law Implementing Regulations (which have preferences in government procurement to national indigenous innovation products), in fulfillment of President Hu's January 2011 commitment not to link Chinese innovation policies to government procurement preferences. See U.S. Department of the Treasury, The 2011 U.S.-China Strategic and Economic Dialogue U.S. Fact Sheet – Economic Track, May 10, 2011.

[105] U.S. Department of Commerce, *22nd U.S.-China Joint Commission on Commerce and Trade Fact Sheet*, November 21, 2011.

[106] U.S.-China Business Council, *Status Report: China's Innovation and Government Procurement Policies*, May 1, 2013, at https://www.uschina.org/files/public/documents/2013/05/innovation-status-report.pdf.

[107] U.S.-China Business Council, USCBC 2012 China Business Environment Survey Results: Continued Growth and Profitability; Tempered Optimism Due to Rising Costs, Competition, and Market Barriers, October 2012, p. 6, available at https://www.uschina.org/info/members-survey/2012/pdfs/uscbc-2012-member-survey-results.pdf.

[108] Foreign Affairs, *China's Innovation Wall: Beijing's Push for Homegrown Technology*, September 28, 2010.

[109] U.S. Chamber of Commerce, *China's Drive for 'Indigenous Innovation' - A Web of Industrial Policies*, February 2011, p. 4.

[110] USITC, China: Intellectual Property Infringement, Indigenous Innovation Policies, and Frameworks for Measuring the Effects on the U.S. Economy (Investigation No. 332-514, USITC Publication 4199, November 2010, pp. 6-7.

[111] See CRS Report RL34292, *Intellectual Property Rights and International Trade*, by Shayerah Ilias Akhtar and Ian F. Fergusson.

[112] U.S. Department of Commerce, *Intellectual Property and the U.S. Economy: Industries in Focus*, March 2012, available at http://www.esa.doc.gov/sites/default/files/reports/documents/ipandtheuseconomyindustriesinfocus.pdf.

[113] Nam Pham, *The Impact of Innovation and the Role of Intellectual Property Rights on U.S. Productivity, Competitiveness, Jobs, Wages and Exports*, 2010, NDP Consulting.

[114] Communications of the ACM, *Who Captures Value in a Global Innovation Network? The Case of Apple's iPod*, March 2009.

[115] The Commission on the Theft of American Intellectual Property, *the Report of the Commission on the Theft of Intellectual Property*, May 2013.

[116] AmCham China, *China Business Climate Survey Report*, 2013, p. 11.

[117] The United States International Trade Commission, *China: Effects of Intellectual Property Infringement and Indigenous Innovation Policies on the U.S. Economy*, USITC Publication 4226, May 2011, p. xiv.

[118] BSA, *Shadow Market, 2011 BSA Global Software Piracy Study, Ninth Edition,* May 2012, at http://portal.bsa.org/ globalpiracy2011/downloads/study_pdf/2011_BSA_Piracy_Study-Standard.pdf.

[119] U.S. Customs and Border Protection, *Intellectual Property Rights, Fiscal Year 2012 Seizure Statistics*, February 2013, available at http://www.cbp.gov/linkhandler/cgov/trade/priority_trade/ipr/ipr_communications/seizure/fy2012_final_stats.ctt/fy2012_final_stats .pdf.

[120] Testimony of Jeremie Waterman, Senior Director, Greater China, U.S. Chamber of Commerce, before the U.S. International Trade Commission, *Hearing on China: Intellectual Property Infringement, Indigenous Innovation Policies, and Frameworks for Measuring the Effects on the U.S. Economy*, June 15, 2010.

[121] AMSC claims Sinovel had obtained the intellectual property from a former AMSC employee who was now under arrest in Austria for economic espionage and fraudulent manipulation of data.

[122] AMSC Press Release, "AMSC Filing Criminal and Civil Complaints Against Sinovel," September 14, 2011.

[123] AMSC, Press Release, April 10, 2012, at http://files.shareholder.com/downloads/AMSC/2346100399x0x558743/f01e0c5a-a526-4102-a818-f61f2d71ef79/AMSC_News_2012_4_10_Commercial.pdf.

[124] "Data Theft Case May Test U.S. China Ties," *Boston Globe*, September 19, 2011.

[125] The JCCT was established in 1983 to serve as a forum for high-level dialogue on major bilateral trade issues.

[126] USTR, *2012 Special 301 Report*, April 2012, available at http://www.ustr.gov/sites/default/files/ 2012%20Special%20301%20Report_0.pdf.

[127] USTR, *2013 Special 301 Report*, April 2013, available at http://www.ustr.gov/sites/default/files/ 05012013%202013%20Special%20301%20Report.pdf.

[128] The White House, *Press Release*, February 17, 2012, at http://www.whitehouse.gov/the-press-office/2012/02/17/ united-states-achieves-breakthrough-movies-dispute-china.

[129] China denies that public officials exert such pressure and that any technology transfers that do occur in China are the result of commercial agreements between companies.

[130] AmCham China, *2012 China Business Climate Survey Report*, March 2012, available at http://www.amchamchina.org/businessclimate2012.

[131] U.S. Chamber of Commerce, *China's Drive for 'Indigenous Innovation' - A Web of Industrial Policies,* July 29, 2010.

[132] However, the Council notes that since the Chinese government maintains approval authority for investment decisions, which may be used by Chinese firms as leverage when attempting to negotiate technology transfer agreements with U.S. firms.

[133] U.S.-China Business Council, *USCBC 2011 China Business Environment Survey Results: Market Growth Continues, Companies Expand, But Full Access Elusive for Many,* November 2011, p. 20.

[134] Inside Trade, *USTR Seeks Info From Manufacturers On Forced Technology Transfer To China,* January 31, 2012.

[135] The report did not identify China (or any country) as the source of the intrusions. McAfee, *Revealed: Operation Shady Rat, An Investigation of Targeted Intrusions Into More Than 70 Global Companies, Governments, and Nonprofit Organizations During the Last Five Years,* 2011.

[136] House Permanent Select Committee on Intelligence, *Chairman Mike Rogers Opening Statement at the Hearing on Cyber Threats and Ongoing Efforts to Protect the Nation,* October 4, 2011.

[137] DNI, Office of the National Counterintelligence Executive, *Foreign Spies Stealing U.S. Economic Secrets in Cyberspace, Report to Congress on Foreign Economic Collection and Industrial Espionage*: 2009-2011, October 2011.

[138] Mandiant, *APT1: Exposing One of China's Cyber, Espionage Units*, February 19, 2013, p. 2.

[139] U.S. Asia Society, Complete Transcript: Thomas Donilon at Asia Society, New York March 11, 2013.

[140] Office of Senator Carl Levin, Newsroom, Bipartisan Group of Senators Introduces Legislation to Combat Cyber Theft, May 7, 2013, at http://www.levin.senate.gov/newsroom/press/release/bipartisan-group-of-senators-introduces-legislation-to-combat-cyber-theft.

[141] Following China's WTO accession, the United States, in January 2002, granted China conditional basis) to ensure that the United States and China had a formal trade relationship under the rules of the WTO.

[142] China generally implemented its tariff reductions on schedule.

[143] USTR, *2013 Report to Congress on China's WTO Compliance*, December 2013.

[144] For an overview of the WTO's dispute settlement process, see CRS Report RS20088, *Dispute Settlement in the World Trade Organization (WTO): An Overview*, by Daniel T. Shedd, Brandon J. Murrill, and Jane M. Smith.

[145] The United States has been the largest target of China's dispute settlement cases in the WTO. Most of these cases have challenged certain U.S. applications of antidumping and countervailing measures.

[146] For additional information about this issue, see CRS Report R43071, *U.S.-Chinese Motor Vehicle Trade: Overview and Issues*, by Bill Canis and Wayne M. Morrison

[147] For additional information on China's restrictions on rare earths, see CRS Report R42510, *China's Rare Earth Industry and Export Regime: Economic and Trade Implications for the United States*, by Wayne M. Morrison and Rachel Y. Tang.

[148] Often, cases are resolved through consultations before a case goes to a panel.

[149] WTO, *Dispute Settlement—Certain Measures Affecting Electronic Payments, Current Status,* August 31, 2012.

[150] A summary of the WTO panel report can be found at http://www.wto.org/english/tratop_e/dispu_e/cases_e/ ds394_e.htm#bkmk394r.

[151] The Appellate Body declared moot and of no legal effect the Panel's findings regarding China's export licensing requirements, minimum export price requirements, administration and allocation of export quotas, and fees and formalities in connection with exportation because of inadequacies in the complainants' panel requests involving these measures.

[152] USTR, *Press Release*, January 31, 2012.

[153] USTR *Press Release*, June 7, 2011, available at http://www.ustr.gov/about-us/press-office/press-releases/2011/june/ china-ends-wind-power-equipment-subsidies-challenged.

[154] Some programs gave tax preferences, tariff exemptions, discounted loans, or other benefits to firms that met certain export performance requirements, while others gave tax breaks for purchasing Chinese-made equipment and accessories over imports.

[155] The GPA is a plurilateral agreement among 41 WTO members (including the United States, Japan, and the 27 members of the European Union) that effectively provides market access for various nondefense government procurement projects to signatories to the agreement. Each member of the Agreement submits lists of government entities and goods and services (with thresholds and limitations) that are open to bidding by firms of the other GPA members. WTO members that are not signatories to the GPA, including those that are GPA observers (such as China), do not enjoy any rights under the GPA. Nor are non-GPA signatories in the WTO generally obligated to provide access to their government procurement markets.

[156] Xinhua News Agency, June 29, 2012, at http://news.xinhuanet.com/english/china/2012-06/29/c_131685154.htm.

[157] Testimony of Karen Laney, Acting Director of Operations, U.S. International Trade Commission before the Subcommittee on Terrorism, Nonproliferation, and Trade, Committee on Foreign Affairs, on *China's Indigenous Innovation, Trade, and Investment Policies*, March 9, 2011.

[158] European Chamber of Commerce in China, Public Procurement in China: European Business Experiences Competing for Public Contracts in China, 2011, p. 15, at http://www.europeanchamber.com.cn/en/publications-public-procurement-study-european-business-experiences-competing-for-public-contracts-in-china.

[159] Inside U.S. Trade, December 8, 2011.

[160] USTR Press Release, December 2011.

[161] *Inside U.S. Trade*, December 12, 2012.

[162] For additional information on this issue, see CRS Report RS21625, *China's Currency Policy: An Analysis of the Economic Issues*, by Wayne M. Morrison and Marc Labonte.

[163] The official name of China's currency is the renminbi, which is denominated in units of yuan.

[164] Much of China's trade is believed to be in U.S. dollars (e.g., exporters are often paid in dollars). The central government requires firms to exchange most of their dollars for RMB.

[165] Calculated from Bank of China data using the official government "middle rate."

[166] U.S. Treasury Department, *Press Release*, December 15, 2006.

[167] The United States is seeking to broaden China's participation in international economic institutions in order to promote the goal of helping to make China a "responsible stakeholder" in the global economy. This implies that, since China greatly benefits from the global trading system and is a major global economy, it should shoulder a greater responsibility in maintaining and promoting that system (rather than just enjoying the benefits of that system.

[168] The United States also pledged that it would review Chinese concerns relating to U.S. restrictions on high technology exports to China resulting from the current U.S. export control regime.

[169] The United States pledged that it welcomed investment from China and confirmed that review of foreign investment by the Committee on Foreign Investment in the United States ensures the consistent and fair treatment of all foreign investment without prejudice to the place of

origin. China promised to revise its Catalogue Guiding Foreign Investment in Industries and encourage and expand areas open to foreign investment, including those relating to high-technology, energy, and the environment. China also pledged to streamline the process for investment approval.

[170] The session was somewhat overshadowed by events relating to Chinese human rights advocate Chen Guangcheng who had been temporarily sheltered at the U.S. embassy in Beijing prior to the session.

[171] CSIS, *Crafting Asia Economic Strategy in 2013*, January 28, 2013, at http://csis.org/publication/crafting-asia-economic-strategy-2013.

[172] The TPP is a proposed regional free trade agreement among 12 countries, including Australia, Brunei, Canada, Chile, Japan, Malaysia, Mexico, New Zealand, Peru, Singapore, the United States, and Vietnam.

INDEX

A

B

C

F

J

K

L

P

Q

R

S

T

U

V

W

Y

Z